WHAT NO ONE *EVER* TELLS YOU ABOUT...

BLOGGING AND PODCASTING

Real-Life Advice from 101 People
Who Successfully Leverage the Power
of the Blogosphere

TED DEMOPOULOS

KAPLAN) PUBLISHING

This publication is designed to provide accurate and authoritative information in regard to the subject matter covered. It is sold with the understanding that the publisher is not engaged in rendering legal, accounting, or other professional service. If legal advice or other expert assistance is required, the services of a competent professional should be sought.

Vice President and Publisher: Maureen McMahon
Editorial Director: Jennifer Farthing
Senior Managing Editor, Production: Jack Kiburz
Typesetter: Todd Bowman
Cover Designer: Design Solutions

Published by Kaplan Publishing,
a division of Kaplan, Inc.

Printed in the United States of America

07 08 09 10 9 8 7 6 5 4 3 2 1

Library of Congress Cataloging-in-Publication Data

Demopoulos, Ted.
  What no one ever tells you about blogging and podcasting : real-life advice from 101 people who successfully leverage the power of the blogosphere / Ted Demopoulos.
    p. cm.
  Includes index.
  ISBN-13: 978-1-4195-8435-0
  ISBN-10: 1-4195-8435-9
  1. Webcasting. 2. Blogs. I. Title.
  TK5105.887.D46 2006
  006.7--dc22

                                        2006026938

Kaplan Publishing books are available at special quantity discounts to use for sales promotions, employee premiums, or educational purposes. Please call our Special Sales Department to order or for more information at 800-621-9621, ext. 4444, e-mail *kaplanpubsales@kaplan.com,* or write to Kaplan Publishing, 30 South Wacker Drive, Suite 2500, Chicago, IL 60606-7481.

Dedication

To my wife, Margaret: Without your support and understanding I may never have finished.

To my children, Jamie, Amelia, and Stacie: Thanks for waking me up early every morning so I could start writing.

To my dog, Tyler, for keeping me company those late nights.

ACKNOWLEDGMENTS

Acknowledgments scare me . . . I'm sure I'll forget someone important. Certainly, my deep thanks and appreciation are due the entire team at Kaplan Publishing, especially my editor, Michael Cunningham, for his patience with me among other things; my wonderful agent, Wendy Keller; and all the 101-plus people who appear in this book!

CONTENTS

PART 3 PLANNING YOUR BLOG 67

PART 4 MAKING MONEY 87

In the past few months I've had a blast gathering more than 101 people's views on blogging and podcasting. I've gotten their views in person, over the phone, over a bottle of vodka in Siberia in the dead of winter, via e-mail, and more. I've talked to a Russian "splogger," or spam blogger, interviewed Silicon Valley executives, e-mailed with Australian entrepreneurs, received great input from celebrity bloggers such as Seth Godin and Guy Kawasaki, and talked to plenty of ordinary people like you and me.

What's amazed me the most is finding expertise in unexpected places. Old friends I've coincidentally reconnected with who had fascinating, and learned, opinions. Tow truck drivers who knew more about certain aspects of blogging for business than I ever will. Surfers with opinions on the future that made me think. The many nonbloggers who consider the blogosphere, the community of all blogs, including the links and social interaction between them, an essential information resource. The levels of passion and knowledge I've encountered across all strata of society have been phenomenal.

What's most impressed me is *why* all these people are passionate: They all benefit directly and concretely from blogging and podcasting. Their thoughts, opinions, and stories are inside. I learned a lot from them, and I hope you will too.

The blogosphere is a massive resource, and you do not need to produce content to benefit from it. Most people don't blog. Most people don't podcast. But many of these people benefit as significantly as those who do. Whether it's by monitoring customers' conversations and perhaps joining them, researching their marketplace and competitors, or keeping up on industry trends and changes, the influence of the blogosphere on the business world no longer can be ignored.

PART 1

THE BASICS

■ ■ ■

Although I first used e-mail in 1979, and was on the Internet for many years before I ever heard the term *"Internet,"* I was a latecomer to the blog party. I started reading a few blogs around 1999, but didn't start blogging until late 2004. I started blogging for two main reasons: to gain more familiarity with the medium, and to reposition myself as a consultant with business and technical acumen instead of as a purely technical guy by writing on both business and technology. I've had a good deal of success on both fronts.

I also had some surprising results. Within 24 hours of starting my blog, The Ted Rap, *www.demop.com/thetedrap,* my search engine rankings for some important terms increased substantially. For example, anyone searching for "Ted Demopoulos" on any of the major search engines would have found my Web site, *www.demop.com,* on the second page of results. Sure, they would have found lots of information about me, such as speeches and seminars I was delivering for some high-profile clients, but not my own Web site on the first page. Suddenly, the number one hit on all the major search engines for "Ted Demopoulos" was my Web site, as it should be. My Web site traffic also blossomed rapidly. My phone started ringing more often. More business was coming my way. I was booking more speaking and consulting gigs. Some new clients specifically said my blog was the factor that made me stand out from competitors. Companies started asking me to help them start blogs and create blogging strategies for them. I was even asked to write a book on business blogging.

Obviously, this is all anecdotal information and I was concurrently involved in other activities to promote my business; however, others report positive results from blogging as well. Podcasts, the audio equivalent to blogs, are also exploding in number and popularity as well, and many report significant business results.

So, what *is* a blog? It's a contraction of the term *"Web log,"* but that's not very informative. How about a podcast? Or a videoblog? What kinds of blogs are there? Why should companies monitor them? What kind of results can a new blogger expect? How are businesses using them?

It comes as no surprise that there are no rules, for these mediums are so new. No one knows where they may lead, and there are no "best practices" or large body of experience to guide us.

There are, though, a number of success stories and experienced people with some well-thought-out opinions. I talked to a lot of them, and 101 of the most interesting appear on the following pages.

1.

WHAT IS A BLOG?

It's just a simple Web site

■ ■ ■

"A blog is just a simple type of Web site that's often updated. That's all it is. Some people go on and on about blogs, often missing the point that it is basically a Web site," says John Raleigh, the co-owner of Raleigh Design and a Web site designer and photographer.

A blog may be more interactive than most Web sites, written in a more personal and conversational tone than most Web sites are, and allow for user feedback in the form of comments, but it's still just a Web site. "Web sites are pretty cool when they're done right," says John. "And blogs make it pretty easy to get it right, so people can concentrate on writing content."

"There is no blog standard, although all blogs are basically the same," continues John. When you look at a typical blog, you'll usually see the name of the blog and maybe a description on top, a number of dated posts, and one or more sidebars that contain related information, such as links to a profile of the author, older posts, and other sites the blogger recommends.

The blog for my own book, *Blogging for Business,* is shown in Figure 1.1—I set it up and John made sure it looked professional by adjusting the layout and colors, and adding a great picture of me. Both I and my coauthor, Shel Holtz, update it.

Notice that it has a title and description on top. The title could be anything, and titles do get rather imaginative and avant-garde, although "a straightforward title is always good for a business blog," according to John. An endorsement appears on top—blogs have a flexible layout, and endorsements are not a common element.

In the left-hand sidebar, you see an invitation to subscribe to the free "BizBlog+ Newsletter," followed by a picture. Pictures and brief biographies of a blog's authors are common.

The wider central column contains the blog's main material, dated "posts" or articles in a reverse chronological format, with the latest post appearing first. New posts are written very frequently, often daily, while the rest of the blog remains relatively static.

FIGURE 1.1 The Blogging for Business Blog, a Typical Blog

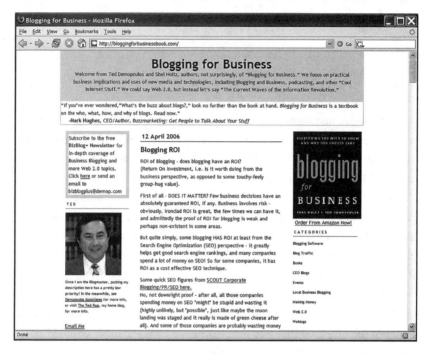

The right-hand sidebar contains another picture, this one of the *Blogging for Business* book, the book that launched 1,000-plus business blogs, as well as a link to buy the book online. Below the picture are categories, which are listings of blog posts by topic area. It's also common to maintain a date-based archive of blog posts.

So if a blog is just a Web site, what is the big deal? "Two things," says John. "Most important, a blog is trivial to update. Adding a new post is as easy as sending an e-mail. By contrast, although updating a Web site isn't rocket science, it's more complicated and time-consuming, and most people hire professionals to do it." That makes a lot of sense. Although I'm very capable of keeping my *www.demop.com* Web site up-to-date, I often hire John for any significant work. "A blog also will have a feedback mechanism," adds John, "often implemented as a way to add comments to posts. The third major difference is that blog posts are written in a personal and conversational manner, unlike the comparatively formal prose of standard business Web sites."

So a blog is just a Web site with a particular format. John, like most Web designers, thinks Web sites are pretty cool, and a "blog is a particularly cool Web site!"

2. BLOGGING IS COMMUNICATING

A blog is a communication channel

■ ■ ■

I asked Randy Barron, "So, what's a blog?" Randy is a resource manager at Axis Technology, LLC, and although he doesn't blog himself, he's been on the Internet forever. I remember getting my first business e-mails from him some 20 years ago. I expected an insightful and interesting answer, and certainly got one.

"A blog is a communication channel," says Randy, "and that's all it is." Blogs complement communication channels we already have, like e-mail, postal mail, traditional Web sites, the telephone, and even face-to-face communications. Blogs are a one-to-many communication channel; the blogger posts and many people see that post. With Really Simple Syndication (RSS), interested people can even register or subscribe, indicating that they want to see all the communications from the blog.

"Blogs are two-way communication channels, and that is a fundamental feature of blogs," Randy continued. "There needs to be some way to communicate back to the blogger. Without a feedback loop, it's simply not a blog." Most blogs allow users to leave comments, and the blogger can answer comments with either another post or a follow-up comment. Not all blogs allow comments, and they are not essential, but there has to be some feedback mechanism. Trackbacks are another mechanism for completing the feedback loop. Trackbacks essentially allow a reader to make a comment on his or her own blog, and have that comment automatically listed on the blog on which the blogger is commenting. "I suppose even publishing an e-mail address in an obvious place and asking for feedback that way would qualify, but that would be less than ideal," Randy added.

Randy believes that "another fundamental feature of a blog is ease of use," and this ease of use leads to the informal and conversational tone of the blogosphere. If publishing a post or leaving a comment was more complicated and time-consuming, more formal conversations would result.

The last fundamental feature of a blog, according to Randy, is persistence. Unlike phone calls or face-to-face communications, blog communications leave a record. You can go and see what a blogger was saying last January, for instance, and what feedback—comments, trackbacks, etc.—he or she received.

Randy believes that too many people concentrate on the current look and feel of blogs. Sure, a blog is implemented as a simple Web site, and typically has a certain format, but those are really details of how blogs are implemented today. They are not fundamental to what a blog is in Randy's mind. Blogs may look and operate very differently in the future, but they will probably offer the same basic communications functionality.

So, in Randy's view, a blog is fundamentally a one-to-many communication channel with a feedback loop that allows two-way communication. Blogs are easy to use, which encourages informal and conversational communications, and the communications have persistence. How a blog is implemented and what it looks like is simply a detail.

3. COMMENTS— ESSENTIAL TO BLOGS?

Most, but not all, bloggers agree

■　■　■

Most blogs allow readers to add comments to individual posts (see Figure 1.2). These comments can be seen by all of the site's visitors and are part of the blog's content. "Comments are an integral component to blogs," says Bryan Person, blogger, podcaster, and professional writer. "They are what give blogs their conversational value."

FIGURE 1.2 Comments on a Blog Post

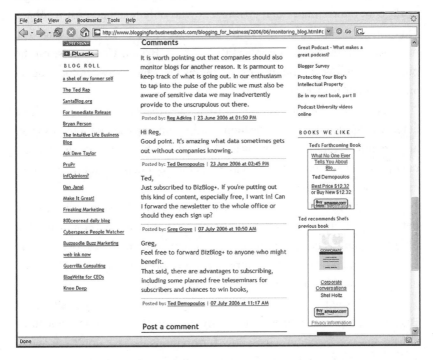

Comments are somewhat contentious. Most bloggers are pro-comment, some go as far as claim that any site without comments enabled is not a blog. Yet some notable bloggers do not feel comments are necessary, or even desirable. For example, popular blogger Seth Godin's blog doesn't have comments enabled, and pioneering blogger Dave Winer doesn't like comments.

Other mechanisms allow reader feedback, such as trackbacks. Trackbacks allow you to comment on someone else's post from on your blog. An excerpt of your text is automatically added to the post you commented on. "Trackbacks are a good way for the blogger and his or her readers to follow the online conversation on other Web sites, and are a very common way for the conversation to spread throughout the blogosphere," says Bryan, "However, trackbacks and comments are two different feedback mechanisms. Trackbacks can only be generated by other bloggers." This is a shortcoming compared to comments, which can be left by nonbloggers and bloggers alike.

Some bloggers accept feedback only via e-mail, sometimes writing a post on an interesting e-mail. "Bloggers who only take and post feedback via e-mail are fully in control of the message, and a one-way message is a monologue rather than a conversation," says Bryan. Comments, on the other hand, allow for a transparent flow of messages between the blogger and his or her readers.

Bryan feels that bloggers need to answer their comments, or at least acknowledge them in some fashion. Follow-up comments by the blogger are a common and immediate way to do this. A blogger may also write a new post that summarizes and addresses the comments to a previous post and perhaps adds a new thought.

Many bloggers moderate comments—that is, the blogger reviews them before they are added and made public. Bryan moderates his comments, but only for spam, such as comments advertising Viagra, and those that are expletive-laden or otherwise unprofessional or inappropriate. However, bloggers should make such moderation policies clear on their sites.

"I don't filter out comments that simply disagree with my posts," adds Bryan. "Doing so would take away my credibility as a blogger. Genuine debate and conversation must allow for opinions that we don't see eye to eye with." Most bloggers don't mind dissenting comments, as long as they are respectful and professional.

Opinions on comments are extremely varied. Bryan's thoughts and practices are quite reasonable, and I agree with him, but each blogger has his or her own feelings and policies. One thing I hate is when I find a new blog with a great post and am mentally preparing a comment, only to discover that comments are disabled on the blog!

4. BLOGGING PLATFORMS AND BLOGGING SOFTWARE

Flexibility or convenience

■ ■ ■

"Blogging platforms and blogging software are two different entities," says Tom Gray of Gray eMarketing Solutions. Blogging platforms are hosted by the blogging company on their servers, and you go to their site and log in to your account to update your blog. Blogging software needs to be downloaded and installed. It can be installed either on the same server as your existing Web site or on another server.

Tom says the advantage to blogging platforms is that "someone else worries about the technical details, including updates to the software." Platforms are usually free or cheap, and you can often start a basic blog in just a few minutes. However, you may have less flexibility. For example, there may be restrictions in your blog's URL, and you may have limited control of its look and feel. Popular blogging platforms include Blogger (*www.blogger.com*), WordPress (*www.wordpress.com*), and Type-Pad (*www.typepad.com*).

Blogger is "blogging for beginners," says Tom. It's free, and you can create a blog in five to ten minutes. "Not a bad place to start but I wouldn't recommend it as a permanent solution," he adds. *Blogger.com* tends to lag behind in functionality, and often it's somewhat important functionality that's missing.

WordPress.com is a popular and somewhat new blogging platform. It's also free and based on the popular open source WordPress blogging software. It's flexible and easy to use, and Tom recommends it. URLs are of the form *myblogname.wordpress.com*.

TypePad.com is another popular choice. It's not free beyond a 30-day trial, although it is quite inexpensive, currently starting at $4.95 a month. Not surprisingly, because it's not free, support is better than with the free blogging platforms. TypePad allows you to map any domain name you like to your blog. *www.BloggingForBusinessBook.com,* the companion blog to this book, uses TypePad.

Self-hosted blogging software is a popular option among advanced bloggers, according to Tom. This provides more flexibility and functionality than a platform, but can also be more complex to use for bloggers who aren't technically savvy or are just starting out. The two most popular software applications are MovableType and WordPress.

MovableType is based on the same code as *TypePad.com,* but needs to be downloaded and installed. WordPress software is often downloaded from *WordPress.com* and is self-hosted. This is similar to the blogging platform *www.WordPress.com,* but it provides users with additional features and flexibility.

For maximum flexibility and ability to customize your site's look and feel, blogging software is the way to go. However, if you want to avoid technical details or want to get started right away, you can start a basic blog in a few minutes on a number of different blogging platforms. If you want the flexibility of self-hosted blog software, but want to avoid technical details, some hosting providers (such as *Yahoo.com* and *Bluehost.com*) will download and install blogging software for you, bringing the best features of each approach together.

5. THE THREE TYPES OF BLOGS

Categorizing blogs

■ ■ ■

Seth Godin is a best-selling author, marketing guru, and "agent of change" who has a successful blog. I'm definitely a Seth fan and ardent reader of his blog, as are a great many people.

Seth has a unique categorization of blogs. He says there are three types of blogs: cat blogs, boss blogs, and viral blogs.

Cat blogs. Seth describes cat blogs as personal idiosyncratic blogs. People who don't know the author may find nothing of interest in this type of blog. But then again, people watch stupid sitcoms on TV, so some cat blogs are very popular. We don't talk much about cat blogs in this book, but here is a hypothetical cat blog post:

> I didn't want to shave this morning because I'm feeling a little depressed. It might be because my wife's doc took her off her medication and she's now nuts and driving me nuts, too. My shrink insisted I can't leave her until she adjusts to being off the meds or her doc has her start back up. Or maybe because I ate so much and blew my diet last weekend—which incidentally gave me HORRIBLE stomach pains all Sat. and Sun. I nearly missed my kid's school play, but my wife's so whacko I went anyway. The play sucked too, except for my son.

Although maybe amusing, do we really want to read this unless we know the author? And if we know who wrote it, even really well, do we really want such detail? Probably not!

Boss blogs. Seth describes boss blogs as blogs for people who work together. The "boss" does not necessarily write them—if there even is a boss at all. Blogs can be amazing tools for communication among a team. They're often not accessible via the Internet, but only on a corporate intranet, so content on boss blogs is usually not public. Here is a hypothetical boss blog post:

> I have a great idea for the Gregory Peccary advertising campaign. Actually, my wife, Samantha, came up with it. It involves a large inflatable mascot—probably some cute furry animal. My daughter, Tabitha, loves it, and she does represent our target demographic. If you remember, Larry, Mr. Peccary himself said small furry animals are nice. I'd like to discuss this approach at our Monday morning meeting if we can . . .

This has several advantages over e-mail. It serves as a permanent record and any comments are attached to it, unlike follow-up e-mail comments, which may be lost, and there is no worrying about who to cc. Also, who needs more e-mail?

Viral blogs. Seth describes viral blogs as ones that want to spread ideas. Viral bloggers have thoughts and opinions and use their blogs to promote their ideas. A viral blog is what most people think of when they think of a blog. Here is a hypothetical viral blog post:

> I just tried an XYZ widget for the first time and must admit I'm starting to understand what all the buzz is about. XYZ users, although maybe small in number, are so amazingly loyal. This is such a great product! It simultaneously helped me lose weight, made me smarter, helped my hair grow back, made me more attractive to the opposite sex, and shined my shoes. More important, it's great in the personalization category. These people really customize the user experience, and maybe with just a few more tweaks will conquer the world, or at least Starbucks. This is a release 1.0 product, after all. . . .

If your target audience is interested in XYZ widgets, this blog post, and your blog, may have significant value to them. Even if they're not yet interested in the topic you discuss on a given day, the fact that your blog is on top of current trends can keep readers coming back to see what's new.

Seth's blog is a viral blog; he uses it to promote his books, workshops, products, and ideas. Many of the blogs that are discussed in this book fit into this category, for blogging for business is all about promoting yourself and your ideas. However, Seth's blog does have some cat blog in it—most effective blogs also contain personal elements and details that give the blog flavor and help to capture the reader's interest.

6. THE VALUE OF BLOGGING

Some concrete reasons to blog

■ ■ ■

Bob Cargill is a creative director and copywriter from Sudbury, Massachusetts, who blogs for some very concrete reasons, as well as because he enjoys it.

First of all, Bob writes his blog, A New Marketing Commentator, *www.anewmarketingcommentator.com,* to keep up-to-date on industry trends, developments, topics, and issues. Being responsible for writing something new at least once a week forces him to stay current and conversant on anything and everything that is related to direct marketing.

"Employers should be extremely happy to have employees who blog. There is enormous value in having employees who not only stay to date in their field but who enjoy doing it and writing about it," says Bob. That should be obvious, but it certainly isn't to many employers!

Bob also writes his blog to build community. Since he began blogging, he has made countless new friends that he probably would not have met otherwise. The blog gets his name and ideas out there and gets him good publicity. Writing a blog is a great way to develop your own new contacts, as well as to bring other like-minded people together. For example, I met Bob through his blog about a year ago, and since then we have met in person and worked together.

When I spoke to Bob, he was on a job hunt for his ideal job. One of his key job-search tools was his blog. He blogged openly and freely about his wants and desires, and he may have found that perfect job by now. And if he hasn't, he has a steady flow of freelance and consulting work, partly because of the extensive network of contacts he has formed through blogging.

A New Marketing Commentator also serves as an ideal staging site for his material, a place where he can post and aggregate his work, which is ultimately propagated and even republished elsewhere. That was Bob's plan from the beginning and is certainly one of the biggest benefits of blogging for him. After he posts his ideas and incorporates feedback from readers, they are sometimes republished as articles in mainstream media publications, giving him a whole new audience. Someday his blog postings may even form the basis for an entire book.

The bottom line is that a blog is a great way to position yourself as someone who has a timely, informed opinion about a particular area—in other words, an expert—and Bob's blog has certainly helped him to do that.

7. WHY SHOULD COMPANIES MONITOR BLOGS?

A wealth of consumer information

■ ■ ■

"Blogs are an unbelievable resource for tapping into the pulse of the consumer," says Julie Woods of Women's New Media. By *consumer,* Julie means anyone who might be interested in typical consumer products, from MP3 players and breakfast cereals to corporate purchases such as network servers and retirement planning services. "Millions of people share their likes and dislikes about products and companies in blogs, opening up a great opportunity to listen to unfiltered feedback," says Julie. "Bloggers give immediate, free feedback without the delay, cost, and restrictions of surveys and focus groups." Companies of any size can gain insight on their customers, competitors, industry, and other emerging issues or trends that may impact future sales.

Anyone can start monitoring blogs with only an investment of time. Plenty of free blog monitoring tools are available, as well as tools that cost up to hundreds of thousands of dollars per year. Julie suggests starting with free tools such as Technorati, Google Blogs, Sphere, Icerocket, and Blog-Pulse. "It's important to use multiple tools because they all monitor millions of blogs, but not the same ones," warns Julie. "There is some overlap, but each tool can also turn up unique mentions." These tools do more than monitor blogs—they offer additional features that can help you understand how influential the blogs are that are mentioning your product or company, and what other blogs are linking to them.

Julie recommends both regularly monitoring all content from relevant blog sites, such as industry- or product-specific sites, and monitoring all blogs for specific terms.

To start, you should conduct a survey for relevant blog sites using free blog search tools. Once you know what blogs to monitor, you need to add their URLs to a feed reader. A feed reader allows monitoring and reading a great many blogs quickly and efficiently for items of interest. Many good free feed readers are available to choose from. My Yahoo! is the most widely used feed reader and is quite easy to use; other free tools that offer some nice functionality include BlogLines, Rojo, and Pluck.

You also need a list of set terms to monitor across all blogs, such as your company name, product names, or maybe executive officers' names. Once you have a list of terms to monitor, you can set up accounts in PubSub and Bloglines to continuously search for mentions of these terms across the blogosphere. You will probably see a lot of irrelevant posts returned initially until you fine-tune your searches.

"For highly visible companies that are getting started with blogging, I often recommend that they start off by working with their PR agency or a blog consultant to develop a blog monitoring and response strategy," says Julie. "The benefit of bringing in outside expertise is that you can jump-start the process quickly." Once you have a monitoring program and tools in place, you can shift over to managing this process with internal resources within a few months if desired. Companies that require an extensive monitoring solution can license products and services from companies such as Cymfony, Nielsen BuzzMetrics, and Umbria. The cost of these sophisticated blog monitoring and analysis solutions can range from $25,000 to several hundred thousand dollars a year. However, this is a relatively small marketing investment for top brands.

Most companies using free tools will take at least two weeks to do an initial survey of bloggers who are writing about their products, company, or industry. This includes investigating well-known bloggers and more obscure bloggers to create a comprehensive list of blogs to read regularly. The next step is to set up feed readers to gather posts from these sites, and then to create search terms to look for discussions about key issues that may come up in the future. This process usually takes a couple of days initially, with adjustments weekly as new bloggers and issues appear on your radar.

At a minimum, companies should expect to have at least one person on their staff spend two hours a day monitoring blogs and responding to comments. Larger companies often employ several staff members or outside agencies to monitor blogs full-time every day, according to Julie.

8. ONE EXAMPLE OF GREAT BLOGGING RESULTS

John Kinde really dove into blogging and
the results show!

■ ■ ■

"My traffic immediately doubled in the first week when I started the blog," says John Kinde, "and it has now quadrupled." John is a professional speaker who specializes in humor skills, and he has been blogging for only three months, but with great success. He is avidly studying blogging techniques and also has a local mentor to help him along.

You might think, "No big deal, he's probably starting from zero," but his Web site has been up for seven years and has been very effective. "It's my main source of bookings. I do no marketing except for my Web site, e-zine, and blog," he says. His Web site not only looks good, but also is well optimized for business on the Web. Many Web sites look pretty, but a nice-looking design doesn't necessarily translate into a site that is built on business experience. I laughed out loud when I first saw it, and because he's a humorist that's high praise. The guy in the next office literally asked me, "What's so funny?" John's traffic is up to 900 visitors each day—from a couple hundred just three months ago.

John is not an old Internet whiz; he describes himself as "starting from square one or maybe square two." He continues, "Wish I had become Internet-savvy years ago. But no time like the present. This is all new to me, and since I've had all my Web site work done by someone else, I guess it's time I've jumped on board and put my own hands into it."

For John, blogging has had benefits besides promoting his speaking engagements. "The great thing, I've learned to enjoy writing," says John. His e-zine, Humor Power Tips, has 2,200 subscribers, a number that's increased significantly since he's started blogging. This is a sentiment shared by a lot of bloggers: They enjoy blogging. They might like the other writing they do, but usually it's considered work—a chore to complete, unlike blogging.

John started his blog, Humor Power, *www.humorpower.com/blog,* with a bang—eight posts in the first two days, and most of them were lengthy. This rapid creation of material helps explain why his traffic grew so rapidly at first. Although he writes an occasional short post, most of them are quite long by blog standards, often more than 1,000 words. He misses an occasional week, but still succeeds.

He's recently added Google AdSense advertisements. The ads immediately started bringing in around $40 a month in added revenue. With his traffic growing and the opportunity to experiment and optimize the advertisements, he's bound to earn much more—probably not enough to get rich, but certainly enough for an occasional night out on the town.

"This is fun stuff. Love it," says John. Equally important, he adds, "and the phone is ringing more!" Blogs have no magical or mystical properties, but sometimes the results seem almost magical. Of course, results will vary and not everyone's results will be as immediately dramatic, but John's results are a great testimonial to the power of blogging.

9. HOW MANY READERS DO YOU NEED FOR SUCCESS?

Blogging and the importance of popularity

■ ■ ■

"Blogging is like being a kid in high school," says Tom Vander Well, partner and vice president of c wenger group. "Basically, everyone wants to be popular." Bloggers are continually checking their Technorati rankings, the number of subscribers to their blogs' feeds, the traffic to their blogs, and so on. There are A-list, B-list, and C-list bloggers, as well as blog subcultures and often a herd mentality.

Being popular may feel good, but it is not essential to success in school or blogging—it depends at least in part on your goals. Lots of formerly popular high school kids are no longer popular and have dull dead-end jobs, while plenty of formerly less popular high school kids are now wildly successful and happy. Sure, high school, like blogging, can be fun, but for some people it's only fun, while for others it leads to increased opportunities.

Likewise, having lots of readers, i.e., popularity, is certainly desirable, but is not required for success. Even if you don't have a large readership, having the right people read your blog can make all the difference in the world. They don't even need to be regular readers. For example, I've had potential employers look at my blog and be positively influenced. Some have told me that my blog has been the differentiating factor, the one that set me apart from other candidates.

Tom gives a great example:

> I occasionally write a blog anonymously just to rant some of my crazier notions. I'm lucky to write a post once a week, have a subscriber rate of one, and precious few people stop by. But I wrote a post a month or so ago and a reporter from Montreal picked it up because it was on topic with a piece she was writing. She e-mailed me asking for an interview. Whouda thunk? It only takes one.

Tom recommends following his mother's sage advice, which is as true for bloggers today as it was when he was in high school:

- **Be yourself.** People want to know you, not just your product or business. Authenticity will serve you well in the long run.

- **The only way to have a friend is to be one.** Don't just listen: comment, post, and join the conversation. It's the only way others will get to know you and what you have to say.

- **Give it time.** Blogging grows organically and exponentially. Slow and steady win the race.

Tom adds, "I wonder how many incredible bloggers with amazing things to share have never gotten past the first few posts." No doubt, many bloggers quit because they feel almost no one is reading their posts. Popularity may be good, but it's not remotely essential to blogging success. Far more important to success is blogging authentically, starting and adding to conversations, and having patience.

10. THE IMPORTANCE OF WRITING WELL

It matters once again

■ ■ ■

"The ability to express yourself in a printed medium has become an important social and business skill," says John Brock, a writer and factory worker. "Writing well is important once again."

Writing was important to our grandparents and previous generations. Writing letters was a critical part of communication for both social and business purposes. The collection of written documents was how history was recorded. For example, the Pilgrims wrote extensively in their journals and letters, which is why we know so much about them. However, journaling died out with the growth of mass media, and the telephone killed letters. Suddenly, writing was not so important.

Large John, as he is known, recollects a beach party in the early 1980s. "This guy who drew portraits was very popular and mobbed by women," he says. "My skill was writing, and no one cared. When I wrote something, I might have gotten my roommate and a couple of friends to read it, at best." There were few opportunities for people who wrote well, but not professionally, to showcase their writing.

"If you think of the Internet as a big beach party, the people who write well command all the attention today," Large John exclaims. "Writing well is important again! We are seeing more and more of this, especially in teens and preteens. When kids come home from school, their social interaction with their peers continues online." For example, when John's 13-year-old daughter comes home, she immediately gets online. She's writing e-mails, posting to her own blog and commenting on others, sending instant messages, updating her MySpace page, and more. Writing is an essential social skill for her. Not being able to write well, or at least adequately, is a social handicap.

Networking is important for business and depends on social skills. A few years ago, most networking was done in person. Today, a major portion of networking occurs online, and is done in writing. Being able to craft expressive e-mails and blog authentically, amusingly, and accurately is important for business and career growth. The appreciation of writing skills, which skipped a generation, is suddenly back and more important than ever.

So, how do you improve your writing? John has a few tips. "Improve your vocabulary," he suggests. "A painter is nothing without his palette of paints. A writer is nothing without his words, and the more you know, the more you have to work with, and the better you can express yourself." The best and most painless way to increase vocabulary is just to read a lot. Large John always has a book going, even if he's so busy he can read only a few chapters a week.

Playing with the language is also important for writing well. Making your prose accessible and even entertaining adds an extra appeal to your blog.

You need to write like yourself, not someone else. "It may sound trite, but every writer of distinction that you have been forced to read over your lifetime gained his distinction, in part, because he reads good," adds John. "There is some quality to his prose that sounds like him. Stephen King sounds like Stephen King. But he doesn't sound like you." You have to find your voice, your style, and once you do, you will write with much more confidence.

Once last piece of advice: "Don't be too proud to give up if you really do suck: Hey—writing's not for everybody." Just like John will never draw portraits well, some people will never be great writers or successful bloggers.

11. DAVE TAYLOR ON SUCCESSFUL BUSINESS BLOGGING

Ask not what your market can bring to you

■ ■ ■

"Ask not what your market can bring to you, but what you can bring to your market," says Dave Taylor, well-known Internet expert and founder of blog training company *BlogSmart.com*. His definition of a successful Web log is one that engages your customers or marketplace, and you can't engage people unless you offer them value.

You need to become part of the discussion. Blogging exclusively about your products simply won't do that, and a blog that concentrates on "you" or "your products" won't do that either. Some people blog only on a given topic and may provide a few links in their sidebar that refer to their products or services. Others will integrate their products and thoughts into their blog entries. Dave suggests that you "can occasionally weave your products into the discussion" successfully, but that it's definitely critical not to overdue it.

Dave considers a business blog as essentially a magazine that you publish for your customers. When I think of a great magazine, I think of one where I become totally engrossed and lose myself for an hour or two. That takes great content, and lots of it. I can easily lose myself for hours on Dave's flagship Web log, Ask Dave Taylor, *www.AskDaveTaylor.com*. I actually called him late for our interview, for I had lost track of time reading his content.

Dave answers readers' questions, primarily those of a technical nature. He sets expectations up front—he can't answer all questions, as he gets between 80 to 150 a day, but he does his best to answer most of them.

"Business blogs should have comments turned on, but moderated," Dave recommends. You exercise editorial control, just like any magazine—it's not censorship. Comments that are not helping you or your customers can be removed without any ethical qualms. Dave deletes an average of two or three comments from Ask Dave Taylor daily. "Hey, it's your business and your blog. You can do whatever you feel is appropriate," he explains.

Market research is important—what are your readers interested in? Dave tracks his questions closely. For example, when he started receiving lots of MySpace questions, he knew it was important to his target audience, and he started researching the site and writing about specific troubleshooting tips related to MySpace. Dave also suggests that it's critical to track search terms people use to find you—terms people type into the search engines. You will often be surprised by what terms people are using to find your site. Dave uses these terms to help him determine which direction to go, what his marketplace is interested in. It's great market research. But Dave doesn't suggest letting popular search terms drive you into areas in which you are not interested. It's also important to track the search terms that are used within your site, if you have search capabilities enabled.

Although he makes substantial money from Google AdSense as well as a few affiliate programs, Dave says that advertising is not for everyone. He does not suggest advertisements for most business blogs. Most business blogs will not generate substantial advertising revenue, so Dave believes that they should concentrate instead on their primary goals, which are usually related to bolstering an existing business.

Engage the customer, provide valuable content, and treat your blog like a magazine. Do whatever is necessary to provide value to your target audience, including figuring out what they want—not what you think they want. Work to weave your products and services into the discussion occasionally, and have fun.

12.

COMMON SENSE
AND BLOGGING

The normal rules of polite conversation apply

■ ■ ■

"Common sense in blogging is often sorely missing," says John Foster, a management consultant who has been making use of the blogging medium since 2001. "Blogging is like speaking in public," says John. "When you speak in public, a few unintended people may hear you, but when you blog, virtually anyone who comes along can read what you've said." If a few bloggers link to your words, you may soon have an audience of a few thousand.

"Blogging is a conversation," adds John, "and the normal rules of polite conversation apply." Often people blog on topics that should remain private, sometimes with predictably disastrous results. They might blog on personal details they wouldn't even discuss with their spouses or best friends, or maybe how they really feel about their bosses and coworkers. There are things that shouldn't be discussed in public, and blogs and the Internet are public. There have even been highly publicized cases of bloggers who were fired for the content of their blogs.

Some people blog anonymously and feel that it gives them total freedom. However, even if you're having a conversation on the street in a strange city, you still might be recognized or overheard by someone who knows what you're discussing. "Similarly, if you are blogging anonymously, it might be obvious to some people who you are," warns John. Don't count on anonymity!

If you write a business blog, you need to know where you stand with your company. Is it an official blog endorsed and associated with the company, or is it independent of your company? If it's an official blog, there may be guidelines or a policy to follow. If your business blog is independent, company guidelines or policies may still apply. If there are no guidelines or policies, use your common sense. For example, speaking negatively about other employees should be avoided, and be wary of unintentionally releasing any proprietary information. Think before you hit publish.

The same rules apply when you are leaving comments on other people's blogs. One difference is that you can delete a potentially offensive blog post you've written, but you usually can't delete a comment you've left on someone else's blog. Also beware that even if you delete a blog post, it still exists. For example, Google caches Web pages, and it may show up in a search. It could also be cached and accessible via the Internet Wayback Machine at *web.archive.org.*

"People confuse how easy it is to blog with freedom from consequences," says John. "No, you can't blog anything you want. The same rules of propriety apply as with any other form of public speech."

13. WHAT IS A PODCAST?

Podcasting 101

■ ■ ■

"Podcasts are more than just downloadable audio," says Shel Holtz, principal of Holtz Communication + Technology, cohost of my favorite podcast (For Immediate Release, The Hobson & Holtz Report, *www.forimmediaterelease.biz*) and my coauthor of *Blogging for Business.*

The biggest difference between downloadable audio and podcasts is the subscription component, says Shel. Podcasts allow you to subscribe, and new shows are automatically downloaded as they are produced. Listeners can subscribe via podcatcher software, an RSS reader that supports enclosures, or iTunes. Regular Internet radio does not allow you to subscribe.

Listeners can also download individual shows if they prefer. Although the term *"podcast"* was created in 2004 from the words *"iPod"* and *"broadcasting,"* Shel stresses, "No, you do not need an iPod to listen to podcasts." Podcasts can be played on your computer or on any portable MPEG player, or even burned onto a CD.

Podcasts usually have a show-like format. They have a host or perhaps cohosts, a theme, and a format. For example, For Immediate Release has cohosts Shel and Neville Hobson. Its general theme is public relations and technology, although they often cover a broader scope of topics. The show starts with its trademark typewriter clicking sounds and guitar lick, ends with music chosen by Shel or Neville, and provides some standard segments, including reader feedback, both audio- and text-based, and perhaps my favorite, Lee Hopkins's report from "down under" (Australia).

The barriers to entry for a podcast are low—they are cheap and simple to produce, especially when compared to radio. No government-allocated and limited radio spectrum is needed. No studio, expensive equipment, or extensive editing are required. Thus podcasts can target niche audiences that would never get airtime on commercial radio stations. Production costs are too high for commercial radio to target small audiences with specialized interests. Shel says he couldn't imagine his podcast on a commercial radio station, because the niche it occupies and the resulting audience are miniscule by broadcast standards.

As podcasting grew, Apple jumped on the podcasting bandwagon in June of 2005, adding podcasts to iTunes and exposing many more people to podcasts. More than 1 million people subscribed to podcasts in just the first few days. In October of 2005, Yahoo! added a podcast directory.

Apple's and Yahoo!'s support has helped attract mainstream media to podcasting. For example, the British Broadcasting Company (BBC), National Public Radio (NPR), and Ebert and Roeper now have podcasts. Some of these are repurposed content, but some are original material created expressly for podcasts. Despite mainstream media's entry into podcasting, independent podcasts are still very popular and growing rapidly, with more than 20,000 independent podcasts currently available.

Some people use the term *podcasting* to refer to both audio and video content. It may sound logical to say that because "video casts are distributed just like podcasts, and iPods now display video, they're all just podcasts," but Shel vehemently disagrees. "I believe we need to be able to distinguish between audio and video. I'd be unhappy if someone referred me to a great podcast, I subscribed, downloaded, and then found out it was video, for which I have far less time, since video requires my undivided attention and I can listen to audio while doing something else."

Podcasting is exploding in popularity. Organizations such as Reuters, *BusinessWeek,* IBM, Virgin Atlantic, NASA, Whirlpool, Cisco, and the

U.S. Pentagon are podcasting. More than 500 new podcasts are started every week, including mainstream media, large company, and small independent podcasts. Podcasting, as Shel has told me many times, is an addictive media, and I'll add it's addictive because it delivers!

14. WHAT IS A VIDEOBLOG?

Vlog anarachy

■ ■ ■

So, what is a *videoblog,* or *video blog,* or *vlog,* or whatever term you prefer? Well, obviously it involves a blog and video for starters. A typical videoblog, if there is any such thing, consists of a blog where posts contain video along with some supporting text.

There has been a lot of discussion about "what is and what isn't a videoblog," says Michael Verdi, coauthor of the book *Secrets of Videoblogging.* Michael argues convincingly that it's a ridiculous question. "Why do we want to define something like this right now? What's the rush?" asks Michael in his classic video Vlog Anarchy, *www.michaelverdi.com/index.php/2005/02/20/vlog-anarchy.* He believes it's too early to define videoblogs. "It's like trying to pick a career and a mate for a newborn, right? It's absurd. We're just at the very very beginning."

Michael says as soon as people decide what a videoblog is, the definition will kill off other possibilities and stifle creativity. "Let's experiment; let's play with the medium. Let's let it breathe and live and grow for a little while before we constrain it with a definition." What distinguishes a videoblog from just a blog with video? Michael would argue that it's too early in the evolution of video and blogs to answer these questions effectively.

What is important and cool about videoblogs is that they "break down the barriers to access to media," insists Michael. Getting exposure on TV or in the movies used to be extremely difficult for people who didn't have connections in the industry. Most people couldn't participate, but that's not the case anymore. In a videoblog, the authors, not Hollywood or anyone else, controls what content is worth producing or distributing. "We get to say," stresses Michael.

"Unfortunately, now that you can do anything, a lot of people are copying existing media," Michael complains. People are copying movies and TV, often right down to its business model, and advertisements in videoblogs annoy him. Videoblogging is about conversations, and no one should interrupt a conversation with an advertisement, he insists. There is a lot of room for creativity in a new medium like videoblogging, and Michael recommends that videobloggers use their imagination—not stay with preexisting video models.

"Let's hold off . . . it's way too early. Let's stop trying to type about what a videoblog is. Let's stop trying to talk about what a videoblog is." Michael insists that experimentation with the medium, not definitions or manifestos, is what's required. "We don't know where this is going to go," Michael believes, and "when we look back on today ten years from now, what will have happened will totally astound us!"

"I don't know what I want, but I know how to get it," sings Johnny Rotten of The Sex Pistols from their classic song, *"Anarchy in the UK,"* as the video ends. Michael may not know what he wants from videoblogging, but he knows how to get there—the continued experimentation of Michael and other videobloggers will lead to the growth of the medium.

15. INTRODUCING SOCIAL MEDIA TO AN ORGANIZATION

Social media hothouse

■ ■ ■

"In late 2004 I got the social media bug," says Joseph Thornley, CEO of the Thornley Fallis Group, a public relations company. Joseph had been experimenting with wikis, Web sites that let any users modify them, as a tool for team sharing of information and for collaboratively creating new documents. During his research, "I came across the concept of RSS feeds—the magic dust that would make blogs as accessible as magazine subscriptions," he adds. "But what to do about it?" His company, like other public relations companies, was firmly grounded in traditional media relations, special events, print publications, and Web sites, and they were good at it.

Joseph decided to introduce social media, media such as blogs and wikis that enable people to connect and collaborate, internally at first, and then roll it out externally. "First, we introduced a wiki alongside our traditional intranet," says Joseph. Eventually, they turned off the traditional intranet completely, substituting the wiki for it; that is, the intranet was essentially replaced by a version that any employee could modify. Joseph also started blogging concurrently, first behind the company's firewall. "Hopefully, by seeing me walk the talk, others would conclude that if the CEO was committed to this, there must be something worth looking at and trying," says Joseph. He took his blog, ProPr, *www.propr.ca,* public in November of 2005.

An internal blog was set up for each employee. "Some use it, some merely comment, but everybody opens their minds to the potential," says Joseph. He expected that the younger generation would jump in first, but actually the older, more senior staff embraced social media first. "Clearly, they had something to say that had been pent up for years and the self-confidence to put themselves on the line," adds Joseph. Several public blogs followed, both by individuals and groups, such as the Web design group's blog, shift+control, *www.76design.com.* Their podcast, Inside PR, *www.insidepr.ca,* started in March of 2006.

After a little more than a year, the entire Thornley Fallis Group has been turned on to social media. They have integrated it into their day-to-day operations, and they are using it and learning from it.

"The payoff—more rapid sharing of information internally and a feeling that our company is a thought leader," Joseph says, "and we have credibility with our clients as they start to awaken to the potential of social media for their communications."

16. IT'S ALL AN EXPERIMENT

There are no experts

■ ■ ■

"Essentially, everything being done these days with social media is still an experiment," says Robert French, who teaches at Auburn University and has worked in public relations for more than 25 years. "It's all still so new. Anecdotal examples of tools and strategies are out there, but nothing that yet works in a multitude of implementations." Many early adopters are passionate and evangelistic, but they sometimes lose sight of logic and reason. I sense passion in Robert for blogs and other social media, but certainly no blind faith. "It's time to sit back and be realistic," he states.

There is no question that Robert is a big fan of social media. He blogs at infOpinions?, *www.auburnmedia.com/wordpress,* primarily for his students and other PR educators and practitioners; he's the "blogkeeper" of Marcom Blog, *marcomblog.com,* which is 15 communication practitioners from around the world mentoring students; and he has his students creating blogs and online portfolios. He uses social media in education in other ways as well, and it has also helped many of his students stand out in the job-search process. "Some have even been hired primarily for their experience with social media," he says.

Robert concedes that search tools truly have universal use and value. They can be used to discover what people are saying about you, your company, and your products. "In-house communication and collaboration via blogs and wikis may be second in line," he adds. And Robert is passionate about social media in the classroom because of the relationships students can develop with experienced people in the business world.

Robert sees people talking and writing about possibilities and implementations with anecdotal results. "There is the usual regurgitation of 'this many people are doing it' or 'here's a big audience' and other such oft-repeated stats," says Robert. But are the numbers real? For example, how many of the 44 million blogs currently listed by *Technorati.com* are abandoned or rarely updated? No one really knows how many people are using or have social media involvement.

"When new tactics present themselves, everyone wants to try and find a way to make them work," says Robert. "There is both the crass aspect of trying to find a new way to bill for something and also the sincere desire to discover new ways to effectively communicate." Robert sees blogs as another tool, another tactic to consider. Blogs and social media supplement, rather than replace, other tools for communication.

"There are no true experts in all of this blogging and social media," says Robert. "The blog explosion is really very young; it has only been within the past two years that blogging has really exploded." Maybe in five years, we'll have solid results we can actually draw conclusions from. Until then, we can experiment and learn; certainly, Robert is experimenting, and he and his students are learning.

PART 2

SOME BUSINESS USES
OF BLOGS AND PODCASTS

■ ■ ■

I thought I was fairly blog- and podcast-savvy. I spend many hours a week blogging and reading countless blogs, both old and valued favorites and literally dozens of new blogs every week. I almost always listen to podcasts while commuting to work and clients' offices, and often explore new ones.

Once I started looking around the blogosphere in a somewhat organized fashion and started interviewing people for their perspectives, I realized I had been seeing only the tip of the iceberg. A lot of creative people are using blogs and podcasts effectively in ways I never imagined.

Lawyers are blogging, real estate agents are blogging, interns are blogging, lots of nonbloggers use blogs for business research, people use blogging to help them learn to write well, blog and podcast media outlets exist, and much more. The stories that follow are from a wide cross section of the blogging world; I hope that their outlooks and ideas will inspire you.

17.

BLOGS AS
SALES RESEARCH TOOLS

An essential resource

■ ■ ■

Jim Foster is a sales professional, and like most businesspeople today, Jim does not blog. Unlike many businesspeople today, he does use blogs as a tool to find information about his clients and prospects, their industries, and even their customers and clients. Jim reads very specific topics and types of blogs, especially before meetings. Before he visits existing clients, he always reads any related blogs, including official corporate blogs and bloggers, as well as the personal blogs of the people he'll be visiting. This brings him up-to-date on what they've been doing or thinking and helps him to continue conversations without a gap from his previous meetings. Sometimes it is clear that Jim has been reading a client's blog or blogs, and although he doesn't mention it up front, his client is often flattered if it comes out. As a result, Jim's stature may be raised from being considered a mere salesperson to a partner who cares about and wants to help the client.

When Jim is about to call or especially visit a potential client, he always looks at the client's Web site first to see if the client has any blogs as part of Jim's information-gathering phase. He also searches using the blog search engines, such as Technorati, to see if any blogs or blog posts related to the company or their products exist. He says that blogs are also a great way to get up-to-date on what is happening within specific industries, and especially if the prospect is in an industry he's not overly familiar with, he'll devote time to learning about the industry and its current issues via industry-specific blogs.

Jim also reads his clients' and prospective clients' blogs between meetings as time permits. This keeps him in the loop and can help him decide and plan when to visit and what to propose in the future. He also leaves occasional comments on blogs as appropriate, and finds that a comment goes a long way in helping a prospective client to remember him. This is also a nonintrusive way of staying on the radar with existing clients.

Jim considers reading blogs to be essential research, similar to visiting company Web sites or reading the newspaper and business press on a regular basis. The advantage of blogs is the information is often more targeted, the tone of the material can be more personal, and he can also hear what consumers and clients of his sales prospects are saying. Although reading blogs certainly provides an advantage, many companies do not have blogs, so Jim often defaults to reading industry-specific blogs and looking for posts on customers' blogs relating to a company or its products.

18. USING BLOGGING TO LEARN TO WRITE WELL

Fulfilling a dream of becoming a writer

■ ■ ■

The phone rang; there was no number on the caller ID, and the woman at the other end insisted that she was anonymous but that I knew her. "You've left comments on my blog," she claimed, "although you have no idea I'm anonymous. I blog under a pseudonym." A crank caller perhaps? I thought, but she was confident and knowledgeable, so I listened.

Anonymous had always wanted to write, "but quite honestly, I was scared, and an atrocious writer!" she declared. She wrote plenty of business documents, but none of that was real writing. It required her only to fill in a form or use the company template. She wanted to write nonfiction and be published, but wasn't comfortable even telling anyone her goals.

About a year and a half ago she started blogging, first slowly, and then profusely. She made up a pseudonym and identity, and blogged her opinions about developments in her industry. Anon felt great doing it, and people were even reading and leaving comments. Not necessarily a lot of people, she admitted, but eventually she had about a hundred unique readers a week.

As she attracted more readers, she became braver and wrote in a more "natural and opinionated style, and people liked my writing and even me better." Her writing improved immensely—she hadn't really written in well over a decade when she was in college, and never felt that she had written more than adequately.

She had a few letters to the editor published in local newspapers. With the first she used her pen name, but the rest were published under her real name. Anon says she "finally got up the nerve to write articles and submit them to newspapers and magazines." The first nine were rejected, but she wasn't surprised. She was writing and loving it. Eventually, she had an article published in a local newspaper. She's followed that up with more than a dozen published articles on everything from parenting to business in the past four months. Three of them have appeared in national publications.

Anon has recently finished a book proposal—she's been working on it for more than six months. She's managed to get a book agent after sending inquiry letters to more than two dozen. She told me that the proposal is being read by several publishers, and she just got her first offer, which was what prompted her call to me.

"I hear you're writing another book—with blogging stories," she said. "Maybe you can use mine. Blogging allowed me to start writing and get people to actually read what I wrote. It was totally pressure-free because no one knew who I was—I even hid my blogging from my husband initially. Blogging built up my writing ability and my confidence, and a lifelong fantasy is now slowly coming true. It's been, and still is, a lot of work, but well worth it."

Anon promises to send me her book when it's published, at which time, at least to me, she'll no longer be anonymous.

19.

BLOGS AS
REFERENCE TOOLS

Turning to the blogosphere for information

■ ■ ■

"Success in my profession is not defined by how much you know, but how quickly you can find what you need to know," says Robert Porter, a software designer and developer. "We've long since surpassed the capability for any individual to have an in-depth knowledge of their chosen field of practice."

Bob finds the general Web valuable, but there is so much information available that it can be difficult to find exactly what you want. "I am truly amazed at how much nonrelevant content is returned in a search," says Bob. He finds another detraction is that a lot of the content tends to be fairly static, not updated frequently (if ever); or conversely, a site may be so rich in constantly changing content that it's impossible to keep up, let alone find what you need quickly.

Bob increasingly turns to the blogosphere for information. Blogs can be, and often are, full of specialized, focused content. There are lots of technical blogs in Bob's field of interest, and indeed, in nearly any field you might choose.

Blogs provide a resource-rich environment that tends to be high in content and low in spurious information, and that provides some degree of interactivity in terms of comments, trackbacks, and other technologies. Bob says that most blog authors will respond to e-mail questions, provided you make it clear you have done your homework and are asking for something they are familiar with.

Another reason Bob chooses to start his searches with blogs is that because blogging takes a degree of effort and commitment, people who blog tend to have something interesting and insightful to say on their particular subject. Over time, blog posts, and blogs themselves, become rich, deep, and broad repositories of detailed information.

Bob typically follows 20 blogs very closely, reading them daily, and "browses" another 40 less regularly. All these blogs are aggregated (collected) for him by Attensa, a plug-in for Microsoft Outlook. Because he already has a huge amount of information in Outlook, including nearly ten years' worth of e-mail, he chose a tool that could bring the content into an environment he's already comfortable searching and using.

He uses familiar Outlook tools to track, categorize, and filter the incoming content. He makes extensive use of the "Search Folders" tool and "Follow-Up" flags to keep track of posts that interest him or he feels warrant closer examination, or that he just knows he'll need to refer to soon. Outlook also allows for any message to be categorized, and he has an extensive category list for blog posts and e-mails.

For instance, recently he needed to know more about SQL server transactions in the ADO.NET data-access model. He searched his Outlook collection, then browsed through the resulting list of more than 200 hits. He categorized the 20 or so that were most relevant as "SQL Transactions" so he can retrieve them with one search later on.

"If I find nothing in my local collection, [which is] rare but it does happen, then I turn to blog-specific searching tools such as Technorati, del.icio.us, Blogdigger, and, of course, Google. While blog entries may not answer my questions fully, they usually will act as a starting point to relevant, prescreened resources on the Web. Blog entries tend to be full of rich context-specific links."

Bob adds, "Don't sell this resource short by any means. Spend some time searching the blogosphere for your areas of interest and you will be amazed at the number of kindred souls out there, or start a blog yourself on your area of interest and watch as people begin to find you!"

20. KNOWLEDGE MANAGEMENT

Shifting gears through blogs

■ ■ ■

"Traditionally, knowledge management has always focused on capturing best-of-breed intellectual capital," says Luis Suarez, a knowledge management consultant with a passion for knowledge management, collaboration, and social networking. Knowledge management refers to how organizations gather, manage, and use their knowledge. It also refers to specific processes and practices organizations use to identify and capture knowledge. This knowledge is sometimes called *"intellectual capital."* In recent years, many large corporations have been spending huge amounts of money to develop and deploy complex knowledge-management systems that allow knowledge workers to share their intellectual capital with others.

"Time and time again, it has been found that these systems failed to provide what they promised," adds Luis. Knowledge workers didn't like using the complex systems, the approval processes in place, and the technical and procedural hurdles that slowed the sharing of intellectual capital. In most cases they had to wait months before the intellectual capital would even become available, at which time it would probably be out-of-date already. These complex systems based on hierarchical control of information frequently failed. Over time, corporations have been realizing that knowledge workers are using their own computers, instead of centralized knowledge-management systems, to store intellectual capital.

Focusing on people instead of tools or processes is a refreshing new way of approaching knowledge management. "Blogs were born to be used as powerful knowledge-management tools," exclaims Luis. "Blogs allow different knowledge workers to have an instant Web presence and platform where they can share with the whole world the materials they have been working on, the intellectual capital they have been building up over the past few months." There is no complex system with a multitude of options, and no wait for a moderator to approve the content as in traditional knowledge-management tools. Instead, blogs allow content to be shared instantly with the whole world. Knowledge workers themselves control the information flow—there is no approval process.

Using blogs has removed the restrictions from traditional knowledge management. Anyone can share content, or intellectual capital, with blogs. Blogs democratize the way intellectual capital flows within the company by putting control in the hands of the knowledge worker. Blogging tools are simple, unlike the complex knowledge-management tools of the past. "Knowledge management has never been so exciting and fascinating!" says Luis. Using blogs instead of traditional knowledge-management tools, the focus and attention is where it should have been all along: on the people!

21. BLOGS FOR LOCAL BUSINESSES

A local business showcases its work through its blog

■ ■ ■

"There is a critical mistake many small and microsize local businesses make when they decide to get themselves on the Internet," says J. D. Iles, owner of the Lincoln Sign Company in Lincoln, New Hampshire. "They tend to fabricate a false Web persona" and try to represent themselves as a much larger company. J. D. almost made this mistake when he purchased the company in mid-2004.

Would people rather deal with a big- box store than with a small family-owned business? Would people rather be customer #0003657 and handle any issues via Customer Relations, which just happens to be in India? J. D. thinks the answers to these questions are obvious.

J. D. blogs at Signs Never Sleep, *signsneversleep.typepad.com,* and has been blogging since August of 2004. "I generally spend from 15 to 45 minutes per day blogging," he says. "This always seems like a lot of time to me, but I enjoy it so I rationalize it as a 'hobby' as well." His blog has absolutely helped him to get new business, and he enjoys doing it and considers it a creative release. It shows him, and his company, as they are: a small personal business.

He first considered blogging for two reasons: First, although J. D. is quite technical, he found it took too long to update pages on his Web site, so he'd get someone else to do it. That meant that the site was rarely if ever updated, and customers would find it "static and dull." Blogging changed that for a blog is almost trivial to update. Second, "The nature of my business sometimes makes it a difficult task to show a customer what we do on a daily basis," and "the nature of a sign is that it goes away pretty quickly once it's finished," says J. D. It's rare for anyone to stop by and see a beautiful completed sign just sitting there.

Blogging helps his business in many additional ways:

- Instead of showing potential customers who visit a photo album or any signs that he may be currently working on, he points them to his blog. It serves as a portfolio of his work. He can direct telephone callers to his blog as well. The blog is in some ways an "automatic salesperson" and can help to make a sale ten minutes later or ten months later.

- He uses his blog to show potential customers sketches of what he proposes. That means there's no e-mail to lose or be eaten by spam filters.

- He uses his blog to keep his customers in touch with the project as it progresses. With his blog, he educates his customers about the sign-making progress as well, and helps them understand that all the work is custom and takes time.

- It's great PR. Customers sometimes share his blog URL with their friends and colleagues.

Lincoln Signs is a small local business that blogs and profits from it. J. D.'s financial and time investment is minimal. J. D. Iles adds, "If you are a small business, be proud to be a small business. Don't hide the fact from your customers. People do not want to do business with companies; they want to do business with other people who they like."

22. INTERNAL BLOGS HELP TEAMS COMMUNICATE

Blogs—they're not just for the public anymore

■ ■ ■

"From early on we wanted a support site for all our bloggers," says Dan Smith, vice president of publishing for the Know More Media blogging network, "but we weren't sure what it would be." They want to communicate lots of things to their bloggers, but they didn't want to spam their bloggers with e-mail, and they also wanted to tap into their bloggers' knowledge.

"It would be really cool to make it another blog and let anyone post to it," they thought, so Know More Media created a password-protected blog for their 45-plus blog authors. Unlike with a traditional support site, any Know More blogger can post to it, and unlike with a typical blog, only Know More Media employees and bloggers have access.

"It's been a really great success," stresses Dan, "and it's surpassed our expectations in terms of creating community and sharing knowledge." Part of the reason for its great success is that all their bloggers see the new posts on the internal blog regularly. When bloggers want to post or see any statistics on their blogs, they log in to the Author's Control Panel, a Web-based tool Know More Media created, and the five most recent posts to the internal blog are automatically displayed.

"Someone is contributing every day," adds Dan. About 70 percent of Know More Media's bloggers posted to the internal blog in the first few months of its existence. It's the only Know More Media blog where there are more comments than posts. When I spoke with Dan, there were about 180 posts and more than 650 comments, so it's clear that bloggers are reading it, thinking, and conversing.

Longer-term bloggers are more likely to post to the internal blog. "Most of our bloggers are not professional bloggers," says Dan. "They have expertise in their specific areas and are learning to blog as they go. That's probably why." So the bloggers with the most to contribute, the ones with the most experience, are the most conversational.

Know More Media has defined about 15 categories for posts to the internal blog. These categories show up in the sidebar, so a blogger can easily click and see all posts in that category. A poster can define a new category for his or her own reference, but it doesn't show up on the list in the sidebar for other users. Know More Media did this to help prevent causing chaos from having far too many categories—very possible with 45-plus people posting—and it is working well.

Blogs are great communication tools. They can be used for external communications over the Internet, as is most common, but can also enable new ways for teams to communicate internally. Dan adds that the best decision Know More ever made was to make their support site a blog, and the second best decision was to give posting privileges to every blogger.

23.

BLOGS AND
PUBLIC RELATIONS

It's not just mainstream media anymore

■ ■ ■

Dan Janal, the founder and president of the PR Leads Article Submission Service and a veteran of the PR industry, believes blogs have changed public relations, although traditional public relations techniques are still alive and well.

"Public relations used to consist mainly of getting press in the mainstream media," says Dan. "Press releases and other pitches were aimed at reporters for print, radio, and TV, and that was about it."

Today, "Mainstream media is dead!" declare some pundits. Of course, mainstream media is not really dead, says Dan, and the traditional press release is neither outdated nor usurped by blogs. However, more people than ever before are going online for information. In some arenas, people don't care if they get their information from ABC, *The Wall Street Journal,* or some blogger named Joe, as long as the source presents interesting information and makes intelligent comments. That blogger Joe might even be a reporter who enjoys being able to write without having his work limited by available space in the local newspaper or altered by his editor.

How do people know that Joe can be trusted to present accurate information along with his interesting and thought-provoking commentary? Simple: Joe has to earn their trust, just as ABC and *The Wall Street Journal* do, and many bloggers have earned that trust among large numbers of people. Many blogs have tens of thousands of visitors daily, and some have hundreds of thousands. Blogs allow anyone to get their message out, and bloggers can present their views of the world complete with audio and video if they'd like. Joe is no longer at the mercy of reporters who may choose not to cover his story or might change his content significantly.

Traditional media, is by definition, mainstream. People with strong or unusual opinions, whose viewpoints are often not represented in the mainstream media, can blog and present their information to those who are interested. Dan blogs and presents his views at *www.prleads.com/blog*. They may not be newsworthy in the traditional sense, but he gets his opinions out to the public and a few thousand people read them.

Dan says that one of the biggest mechanisms for growth in the blogosphere are links and related trackbacks. When someone links to another's post, it's often a voice of confidence: "Hey, check this out—this is worth noticing." Trackbacks have a similar effect. These "votes of confidence" can quickly bring increased visibility to a blogger's views, just as the mainstream media can bring increased visibility to the content of a press release by publishing information from it.

The blogosphere is an egalitarian space, and most bloggers can be contacted easily. Their blogs often include personal e-mail addresses or, in some cases, telephone numbers, even for some of the most popular bloggers. Almost all blogs allow conversation through comments. Readers without blogs can contact a blogger if they have something interesting to point out, and the blogger just might chose to blog on it. Sending a blogger a press release isn't a great idea, however—it's all about personal contact, and a press release is about as impersonal as you can get.

Dan reiterates that mainstream media, traditional PR, and the press release are not dead. However, blogs offer an alternative and a more egalitarian channel for public relations.

24.

BUILDING GREAT BUSINESS RELATIONSHIPS THROUGH BLOGGING

Networking through blogging

■ ■ ■

"Blogging is a natural relationship builder," says Phil Gerbyshak, author of the book *10 Ways to Make It Great!* If you are blogging about your profession, then many of those relationships will be with people who work in your field or in a related area.

"Comments are very important," says Phil. More traffic doesn't necessarily lead to more comments or conversations—they are not directly related. Phil prefers comments by far to more traffic. "If someone has taken the time to comment, send them an e-mail and say 'Hi' and 'Thank-you,'" suggests Phil. If the commentor is another blogger, he or she probably has an "About Me" link somewhere on his or her blog. Take the time to visit the commentor's site before responding. You might find that you have additional interests or contacts in common.

Sometimes bloggers almost seem to hide their "About Me" links. Phil recommends you display yours prominently, keep your information up-to-date, and have an e-mail address available. If you're paranoid about displaying your e-mail address, then open a free e-mail account specifically for blog-related e-mail and check it once a day or so.

Phil also likes to interview some of the people who leave comments on his blog, Phil Gerbyshak Challenges You to Make It Great!, *makeitgreat. typepad.com*. Often he'll post a short e-mail interview on his blog, and those posts tend to result in significant traffic. Most commenters are also bloggers and will often link to the interview as well.

Make sure you respond to all your e-mails and trackbacks. For a typical blogger, this is not a lot of work, but it is often greatly appreciated. Sometimes a simple "Thanks for the link" or a similar message is all it takes.

"Blogroll for sure," says Phil; that is, have links to the blogs you have connected to displayed on your blog. You don't need to link to everyone who contacts you, but certainly to people you have relationships with or whose sites are relevant to the topic your blog discusses.

Phil suggests you extend your relations beyond just blogs. We've already mentioned e-mail, and you can also use online address book services such as Plaxo or social networking sites such as LinkedIn. LinkedIn and some others are particularly interesting as you look inside other people's networks.

"Bloggers like to help other bloggers," says Phil, "and that makes it easy to network and make connections." Networking skills from blogging often transfer to other situations as well; we don't blog in a vacuum. Phil recommends you take what you learn as a blogger and apply it in life. "There are lots of experiences to help you grow as a person," adds Phil.

25. POSITION YOURSELF AS AN EXPERT

And keep building your expertise

■ ■ ■

"You need no one's permission to start, and can blog on any topic you are passionate about," says Becky McCray, an entrepreneur who blogs on issues for small businesses in rural areas and small towns at Small Biz Survival, *www.smallbizsurvival.com.* She grew up in rural west Oklahoma and loves it. Unfortunately, the population in Becky's area, and in similar areas across the country, has been declining for decades. She has a background in economic development, but "not very many people locally thought of me as an expert," she says.

Becky believes you should state your purpose, topic, and approach early on.

"I started with a sheet of paper and wrote a few bullet points, defining what I saw as the overall theme of economic development and small business tied to my interest in small towns," says Becky. That was the basis of her first post, explaining her purpose in blogging. "It also served as a good reminder for me of what I wanted to target."

Becky suggests that new bloggers link to work by established sources, and add your thoughts. "I started by just copying and pasting whole stories with a link to their source, and maybe a short comment," she says. She still does that occasionally, but she also tries to add some new content that will be of real value for her readers.

"You also need to write original stuff," Becky says. "If you don't have anything original to add, you may not be an expert." You can reuse workshops, handouts, articles, or tips you have already written. She looked through old material she had written and used once, and used this material as the basis of many blog posts she could share with the world. You can also reuse your blog writings as new workshops, handouts, articles, and tips.

"Tell others in your network and industry about your site, especially non-bloggers," suggests Becky. You can get their feedback and encourage them to refer others. You might even be able to get them to write a guest article.

"Add to conversations on related blogs," Becky recommends. "Sometimes I would just comment on the original post and leave a link. Sometimes I would comment and start a whole new post on my blog," says Becky. She seldom leaves "Yeah, I agree" type comments, as they add little value.

Becky recommends entering carnivals, which are a "best of" list of posts on a certain topic. Carnivals continuously move to new host blogs, hence the "carnival" aspect. She has entered Carnival of the Capitalists, Carnival of Entrepreneurship, Carnival of Marketing, and Carnival of Business. "Every time, I have received a boost in the number of people who read that particular article, and it also boosts my general subscribers," she says.

Becky suggests you list yourself as the author of your blog, for example, "Becky McCray, author of Small Biz Survival," and include it in your bio.

It's also important to treat yourself as an expert. Maybe no one in the offline world thinks you are an expert yet, but build your expertise. Experts who don't build their expertise don't remain experts for long. Becky adds, "While you are writing your stuff, you are making yourself into an expert. You are improving your knowledge and understanding as you research articles, read related materials, and keep up with industry thinking."

26. BLOGGING FOR BUSINESS RELATIONSHIP QUALITY

Not all clients are created equal

■ ■ ■

Robert Rosenthal is the founder and creative director of Mothers of Invention, a direct marketing agency. The company's Web site, *www.themothersofinvention.com,* makes it clear that it's not a typical agency. Along with the traditional "About Us" link, there is an "About You" link. The "About You" page begins with "You consistently treat people with respect. Prefer collaboration over command and control. . . . Mean what you say." It's as if the agency is saying, "If this doesn't describe you, then we don't want you as a client."

"There are too many toxic relationships in the marketing field, and I'm looking for the healthy ones," says Robert. "The ones that are supportive rather than dysfunctional, collaborative versus competitive." His Web site helps dissuade clients who tend to have bad relationships. Robert's blog, Freaking Marketing, *www.freakingmarketing.com,* takes it a step further.

From the name, Freaking Marketing, to the content, it's very clear you're not hiring a yes-man or a yes-firm. Robert's personality shines through in a strong, authentic, and accurate way. It's pretty clear that you don't hire Robert's creative firm to take orders—he sees that as a conflict with the agency's mission of creativity.

Robert blogs about direct marketing successes and failures. He uncovers dirty laundry—things marketing firms do he feels are unethical. For example, in a recent post, he discusses agencies that "call a mediocre advertising campaign or corporate identity program a 'brand-building campaign' or 'branding initiative'" and charge dearly for it. Robert also blogs about bad client relationships. In his post *Do As I Say—Then I'll Fire You,* he discusses autocratic rulers with zany commands and plans that will probably fail miserably. Robert is proud that a friend fired a terrible client after reading this post!

"A bad client can be a major drain on its agency. By generating unexpected, pointless, time-sucking busywork, agency people have less time to devote to good clients," Robert says. "When a bad client pulls a stunt that makes agency members feel dispirited or pissed off, they become distracted for at least a brief period."

Robert is going to be busy no matter what. He's highly competent and has a superb track record, and a strong following. Having impressive clients who pay big bucks isn't so important to Robert as working for good people and getting stellar results. His blog, easily accessible from his company's home page, dissuades clients who are not a good fit. His personality shines through on his Web site and especially on his blog. If you don't like it, you're not likely to work with Robert, and that's better for everyone involved.

27. BLOGS AND PODCASTS AT 800-CEO-READ

A media source based on blogs, podcasts, and more

■ ■ ■

At first glance, 800-CEO-READ is an online bookseller that is passionate about business books, but "we look at ourselves as a media source," says Todd Sattersten, vice president of 800-CEO-READ. They publish their own opinions as well as the opinions of authors and other thought leaders.

"We've been doing this for two years and we think it's very important," adds Todd, referring to their blogs, podcasts, and other editorial content on the Web. 800-CEO-READ needs to differentiate itself from others who sell books online, including larger retailers such as *Amazon.com.* They do this quite effectively in a couple of ways: They have their own niche—business books—and they provide a level of information about these books that is not available anywhere else. Their Web presence includes their Web site, blogs, and a podcast, and is more like a television show or magazine than a brochure.

Their first blog, now well over two years old, is their Daily Blog, *www.800ceoread.com/blog,* a multiauthor blog that contains news about business books, links to reviews, their own reviews, their top 25 books, and authors who guest-host the blog occasionally. Their Excerpts Blog, *www.800ceoread.com/excerpts,* runs excerpts of popular business books. Their podcast, *www.800ceoread.com/podcasts,* offers interviews with authors, excerpts of audio books, and more.

Their InBubbleWrap blog, *www.inbubblewrap.com,* is very interesting, popular, and extremely innovative. It is completely advertiser-driven and based on paid placements. It features books and occasionally other business-related products—one item per day—and has daily contests for free merchandise. As I write, today inBubbleWrap features the book *Treasure Hunt, Inside the Mind of the New Customer,* and several lucky readers will get free copies.

The last part of 800-CEO-READ's media strategy is ChangeThis, *www.ChangeThis.com,* which although blog-like, is not strictly a blog. ChangeThis features "manifestos" written by thought leaders and authors, and "is aiming to disrupt the media pattern with powerful, rational arguments from leading thinkers." The site has more than 4,000 subscribers to its RSS feed, and more than 14,000 readers receive notices when new manifestos are posted. Recent manifestos include "111 Ridiculously Obvious Thoughts on Selling" by Tom Peters and "Citizen Innovator" by Eric Von Hippel. Anyone can submit a proposal for a manifesto, as well as vote on which proposals they like. Of course, there is a ChangeThis manifesto that talks about the mission of the site itself.

800-CEO-READ is a media source that uses a combination of a Web site, several blogs, a podcast, and ChangeThis to publish content they feel passionately about. Their passions include business books, and they use these communication tools to provide an unparalleled level of information about the books they sell.

28. BLOGS HUMANIZE COMPANIES

Microsoft, part I

■ ■ ■

"It's striking how much blogs have positively changed my impression of Microsoft," says Jeff Foster, vice president of development at Symmetric Technologies, Inc. Microsoft's blogs have made a "drastic difference" in how he views Microsoft, and many others agree. These blogs have helped humanize Microsoft to thousands of software professionals like Jeff.

Jeff deals with Microsoft technologies every day, and new technologies and changes to old technologies can dramatically impact his business. Microsoft's image used to be that of an "imposing and impenetrable monolith that was secretive and nasty," says Jeff. A quick Google of "Microsoft evil" brings up more than 2 million hits, with the top hits commenting on "heartburn, acid reflux, and peptic ulcers," "Microsoft buys evil from Satan for 2.7 billion dollars," and "Microsoft's Army of Evil Monkeys."

Something has happened fairly recently to "Microsoft's Army of Evil Monkeys"—they started blogging en masse, and suddenly they seem less evil. They actually seem human—a bunch of human technologists totally engrossed in what they're doing, and doing the best they can to bring out top-notch new technologies and products. And they are read by another bunch of technologists: technical users of Microsoft technologies who have realized they have a great deal in common with the supposed "Evil Monkeys." Readers are finding that they have many similarities to Microsoft bloggers, despite differences in geography and in the size of the companies they work for.

Jeff Foster has started reading several Microsoft blogs, including the Channel Nine video blog, *channel9.msdn.com,* which features unplanned and unscripted short interviews with key Microsoft technologists. For the most part, readers don't check these out to see Microsoft's human side; Jeff and thousands of others do so for the great technical information and opinions, much of which is unavailable elsewhere. In the process they see that, in Jeff's words, Microsoft is "less of an antagonistic marketing entity and really just a bunch of guys doing technical stuff they're really into." In fact, Jeff laments that he doesn't have more time to read Microsoft blogs and watch Microsoft's Channel Nine videos.

One key benefit of blogs for large companies is that blogs can humanize them. They give a company a voice and a face—or, like Microsoft, many voices and faces. A company becomes a group of people instead of a faceless corporate entity. People can relate to and trust other people, while no one really relates to the abstract image of a company.

A few large companies have taken advantage of the humanizing effects of blogs. General Motors is no longer a faceless monolith because of the blogging efforts of Vice Chairman Bob Lutz; Boeing is represented by Randy Baseler; and Sun Microsystems is represented by Jonathan Schwartz. You might well ask, "Who cares?" Besides the companies involved, people working with or interested in cars, airplanes, and computers care, respectively.

"Who cares" about a large company's blogs and their humanizing effects? People who care about the company's products. Most people don't care about Microsoft's blogs except the people most important to Microsoft: those building business solutions with their technologies and products, people like Jeff Foster.

29. BLOGGING FOR A BIG COMPANY

Microsoft, part II

■ ■ ■

Jeff Foster told us how positively blogs have changed his perception of Microsoft, so I thought I'd see the view from inside the Microsoft corporation. Microsoft has well over 3,000 bloggers, roughly 5 percent to 6 percent of the entire company, and many additional employees read and comment on these blogs. Clearly, Microsoft's corporate culture has embraced blogging.

So how and why did this massive wave of blogging start at Microsoft? Microsoft decided it was OK for employees to talk directly to customers—in fact, they decided that they couldn't afford not to have employees and customers talking, and blogging is a highly effective way of communicating. "A few years ago, management made it clear that blogging was OK," says Alfred C. Thompson II, an academic relations manager at Microsoft and an avid blogger. Of course, some blogging was already going on. Eric Rudder, a well-regarded senior executive at Microsoft, leading by example, started a blog, and blogging took off at Microsoft, relates Alfred. Having a high-level person such as Eric blog was instrumental. Extremely popular technology blogger "Robert Scoble joining Microsoft was a big factor, too," adds Alfred.

Alfred jokes that "Microsoft was never as evil as people thought it was, and it's less evil now," and comments that all entrepreneurs have a competitive, maybe even mercenary, streak to them. By having employees directly communicating with customers, Microsoft lets customers see that its employees are simply people passionate about, and happy with, their work. Also, employees can produce better products and solutions for customers if they know what the customers' needs and desires are firsthand.

Why are Microsoft blogs so successful? Well, passionate bloggers tend to be successful bloggers, and, Alfred adds, "I don't think you can get a job at Microsoft if you're not passionate." Microsoft employees tend to be not only passionate about what they work on, but have other passions as well. These passions start from the highest levels: Bill Gates is passionate about bridge and philanthropy; Steve Ballmer is passionate about running and basketball. "The noninteracting geek is a myth," according to Alfred.

"Most bloggers at Microsoft think of themselves as bloggers who write about their work, which they find interesting. The fact that they work at Microsoft is a detail," says Alfred. "Most of them would still keep blogging if they left Microsoft."

So, what will happen in the future? Well, Microsoft employees will keep blogging in greater numbers most likely; between August of 2005 and April of 2006, the number of Microsoft blogs hosted on *blogs.msdn.com* and *blogs.technet.com* grew from 2,000 to 3,000, and that doesn't even include all Microsoft blogs. Also, technology is a volatile industry—people move around. Former Microsoft employees are likely to bring blogging en masse to their new companies as well.

30.

CREATING BUZZ WITH BLOGS

Getting your message out

■ ■ ■

"Blogging is one of the best ways you can get your authentic message out," says Ron McDaniel, CEO of Buzzoodle, word-of-mouth marketing. "No fancy marketing, no carefully worded Web pages, just an honest and personal look into the people within an organization, or at the individual writer." It's no surprise that one of the primary ways marketing agencies measure buzz and word of mouth is by monitoring the blogosphere.

"Unless you are a big celebrity, a blog does not get you buzz right out of the gate," adds Ron. It can take months of blogging several times a week before you get an audience big enough to matter. You can attract an audience more quickly by posting often and using many of the other techniques in this book.

Blogs create buzz because people will feel like they know you, and people like to do business with people they know. They will care about your success and will talk about you, write about you, or invite you to speak.

Ron recommends that large organizations consider getting multiple people in the organization to commit to being experts on various fields and posting a certain minimum amount, tying what they are writing back to the company at least a little. For such a blog to succeed, companies must allocate time to blogging and promoting the blogs. "With this approach, over time you will develop a significant amount of buzz," says Ron. "Your company will be seen as a company full of industry experts." You'll also generate significant content that will draw more people into meaningful relationships with you. Your employees will be invited to speak, participate in roundtables, write articles, and more. These employees may not be members of the sales department, but eventually they may become your top lead generators.

Creating buzz is a backdoor approach to sales—you don't ask for the sale. Instead, you cultivate an audience of people who ask you to sell them something, or they go out and sell on your behalf. "Whether you are using one blog to establish yourself as an expert, or many blogs to establish a company full of experts, the expert status and buzz a blog will help you achieve will transform your organization," says Ron.

It's easy to be skeptical, but blogging will work if you work at it, provide quality, and promote it. Ron's results with Buzzoodle are illustrative. Buzzoodle's biggest prospects, including several Fortune 100 companies, contacted him because of the Buzzoodle blog, *www.buzzoodle.com.* Ron has been invited to present at conferences, write articles, and contribute to books, and people have asked to advertise on the blog. "My dirty little secret is that I have only been blogging since 2005 and I was a tech person when I started," says Ron. "Now I am an internationally recognized word-of-mouth and buzz marketing expert. All thanks to the blog."

31. MARKETING WITH CONTENT

Don't interrupt people;
instead, attract them with value

■ ■ ■

"Content on the Web is the best form of marketing there is," says David Meerman Scott, author of the book *Cashing in with Content* and a professional speaker. Although David refers to all types of content, including Web sites, blogs, and podcasts, he's not talking about information about your product or marketing messages. He's referring to content that provides value.

All marketers are looking for ways to find buyers, but most use interruption marketing. For example, a television ad interrupts a show and tries to get the viewer to continue watching. We are subject to countless marketing interruptions every day, and they are no longer as effective as they used to be—there are too many of them!

Marketing with content is radically different than traditional marketing, such as telemarketing, print and television advertisements, and trade shows. Marketers often forget that the main reason people use the Web is for content. Content is not forced on people; they access it because they want to. Search engines organize content, make determinations about its relevance, and direct more people to it.

Instead of running traditional ads for your brand of vitamins, for example, you could provide lots of information on vitamins on your Web site— why they are good for you, different types, etc. Consumers interested in vitamins are likely to find and read your information. Some of them will buy your vitamins and hopefully become long-term customers.

By making useful and valuable content available, a site can come to be seen as a trusted resource on a given topic. "Getting thoughts out there brands you or your organization as intelligent. It's truly amazing," says David. "People think, 'They have great ideas. I might want to do business with them.'"

Blogging and podcasting take content marketing one step further as they encourage conversation around the content. Links, comments, and trackbacks are a forum for discussion around content, moving into the sphere of viral or word-of-mouth marketing.

At the end of 2005, for instance, David wrote a short e-book called *The New Rules of PR*. His work was primarily consulting, but he wanted to get more paid speaking gigs. Writing his e-book was a minor effort for most of it relied on content he had previously written.

In January of 2006, he released the e-book via his blog Web Ink Now, *www.webinknow.com,* and received moderate traffic. Four or five bloggers linked to him and he had about 2,000 downloads. On the fourth day, popular blogger and author Seth Godin linked to him and David had 8,000 additional downloads. Two days later, another popular blogger, Steve Rubel, linked to him with somewhat negative comments. "Suddenly, there was controversy, and a fat loud conversation going on," David recalls. In the next month, he had 50,000 downloads, and six months after his book's release, 75,000 people had downloaded his e-book. He booked ten paid speaking engagements, got new consulting clients, and saw an increase in the sales of his earlier books.

This took a fairly minor marketing effort on David's part. It cost next to nothing and had major results. Imagine the expense of reaching 75,000 targeted people via conventional marketing—it might have cost a million dollars. This example really illustrates the potential payback of content marketing. "Content marketing is a fabulous form of getting your message out there," says David. "Marketing with content works, and it's going to explode."

32. BLOGGING INTERNS

Building skills, confidence, and networking

■ ■ ■

"It's a great experience," says Christopher Salazar, a Web and marketing intern with a Global 1000 technology company and a marketing major at Santa Clara University, referring to both his internship and his blogging. Christopher started blogging shortly after starting his internship, encouraged by his manager and mentor, and has seen numerous benefits.

Christopher posts at least three times a week at his blog, e-Bizz by Christopher Salazar, *ebizz.wordpress.com.* He spends three to four hours a day blogging, including the time he spends reading other blogs and leaving comments. Christopher uses blogging to keep up with current events in business and technology. He even wakes up early to see what's new.

"My school says network, network, network, but doesn't say how," says Christopher. One of the advantages to blogging is social—the networking. Through blogging, he's connected with lots of people in the business world, both online and in person at local blogger dinners. Blogging is an ongoing networking tool.

Christopher's confidence has increased significantly. "The fact that I'm thinking 'Business' more often is a big help," he says. "Blogging makes you look at things in a more analytical light." He's learned the importance of critically analyzing things, which is what he does at work all the time. He says that his studies address nonreal world "word problems," while blogging and business is "real-life analysis." "It's also amazing how my writing skills have improved since I started blogging," Christopher adds.

Christopher is looking forward to his transition in a few months to the full-time business world. He's built confidence, skills, and a network through blogging. He actually wants potential employers to Google him and see what he's been doing! Along with his MySpace and Facebook information, almost a given for a student, they'll see all the critical thoughts, analysis, and opinions that appear in his blog.

33. BLOGGING AND YOUR CAREER

Career advancement through blogging

■ ■ ■

"My primary motivation was to hopefully build my professional reputation outside of my IBM circle," says Philip Hartman. "Developing such a reputation in the industry is an important consideration for me to get my next promotion at IBM."

Philip was no newcomer to blogging. He began blogging in his personal life well over a year ago as an outgrowth of keeping a personal journal. "I found I liked writing more than I expected and began to look at blogging as a 'better journal,' in that someone else might read something that I was going through, could potentially benefit, and we could potentially interact even though we'd never met," adds Philip.

Then something interesting happened: His employer, IBM, like a few other companies, began to openly encourage employees to blog. They published a blogging policy requiring only that employees not reveal proprietary information and that they include a disclaimer stating that the opinions were their own and not IBM's. Because Philip was already blogging and enjoying it in his personal life, he decided to "bravely embrace the challenge and begin blogging about my professional life as an information technology architect [who] helps clients solve business problems with computer technology." He began his blog, The Art and Science of Being an I/T Architect, *artsciita.blogspot.com.*

"I've posted about the impact of corporate culture on technology investments, what various technology trends mean to me, the changing role of the Information Technology professional as more and more work is sent offshore to India and other lower-cost countries, professional certification, business issues, career advice, what others are saying, business problems, impact of government regulation, and more," says Philip. Sometimes he gets permission from other IBMers who aren't blogging to publish their thoughts, being sure to give them credit, of course.

Philip has been pleasantly surprised to find that many of his peers have found his "humble blog," as he refers to it, and keep coming back. In particular, he has a lot of readership overseas from people he otherwise never would have met. He's also been amazed at how high his blog ranks on Google and other search engines. For example, he calls himself an "I/T architect," and his blog is currently the number one ranked site on Google for that search term. He also ranks high on many other search criteria, and the search engines drive readers in his target audience to his site.

It's quite clear he's reaching his goal of building his professional reputation outside of his IBM circle and becoming well known in the industry. And it's also obvious that he's enjoying himself in the process. "All in all, I've really enjoyed my time in the blogosphere," says Philip, although he admits that his wife thinks he spends too much time blogging. Philip likes blogging and he's passionate about his topic. It's no surprise his blog is successful!

34.   BOOK BLOGS

A low-cost, high-impact tool

■ ■ ■

"It's a low-cost, high-impact marketing tool you've got to have," and "you shouldn't do without it," says Michael W. McLaughlin, coauthor of *Guerrilla Marketing for Consultants*. Michael is referring to a book blog, a companion blog to a book. And as you can tell from the title of Michael's book, he knows a lot about marketing.

Michael's book-related blog, *guerrillaconsulting.typepad.com,* Web site, and newsletter all came out in late 2004. His blog experiences have been very positive and very well received—far more than he expected. He won a MarketSherpa award for best business-to-business blog, he receives a lot of feedback, surprisingly more via e-mail than in comments, and he's met many interesting people. In general, readers don't contact authors— they don't even think about it. "A blog makes you seem more approachable and people feel much more comfortable contacting you," says Michael, and he's been contacted for lots of speaking events and other writing opportunities. Having a book blog, sometimes called a *blook,* brings the reader and author closer together.

Many book authors start Web sites and blogs to sell additional products such as e-books, audio products, or consulting. Michael's goal was different: He wanted to extend the conversation in the book, and he's succeeded, both through the blog and through people contacting him directly. His book is a finished piece of writing, but it's not "done"; it lives on through his continued blogging, and roughly 300 to 400 people daily read his blog.

Michael and coauthor Jay Conrad Levinson covered the usual bases for book promotion; they hired a publicist for two months, used their mailing lists, let professional service provider organizations know about the book, and built the book Web site and blog. They did most of the promotion themselves and didn't spend much money. The most effective technique? Probably blogging. "My sense is it worked better than anything else," says Michael, although he has no hard statistics. He also says his Amazon sales ranking for the book, something many authors obsess over, is higher when he is blogging more frequently: "There seems to be a direct relationship." He often gets feedback from people who buy the book after finding and reading the blog first.

What would Michael recommend to a new author?

- The publisher is not going to market your book for you. Success is driven by what you do.

- You want to build staying power for your book and push hard in the first 90 days to 6 months after its release.

- Take advantage of the intellectual capital in the book. Expand, update, and take it in other directions, and do something with all the great material you wrote that didn't make it into the book.

Blogs can be useful in all three of these areas. Michael's story shows that a book-related blog can help boost sales and bring the book to new audiences. A book blog also gives you the opportunity to keep readers interested by providing them with new material that's related to the topics you cover in your book.

What would Michael do differently if he were starting now? He would certainly need to look at blog tools carefully—they have all evolved since he's started blogging. He might start just a blog instead of a blog and a Web site. As far as the actual blogging is concerned, he modestly says he doesn't know enough to determine what he might do better or differently—but the results he's had so far show that he does know what he's doing.

35.

A BLOG AS
A WEB PORTAL

Providing information to customers

■ ■ ■

"Our blog, GMP Training and Implementation Tips, *www.gmptraining systems.blogspot.com,* is designed to provide timely and useful information to people working in the FDA-regulated industries," says David Markovitz, president of GMP Training Systems, Inc. "GMP stands for Good Manufacturing Practice and is the regulation guiding the manufacture of pharmaceuticals, medical devices, biologics, cosmetics, and foods." David also gives talks on the evolution of food and drug law during Teddy Roosevelt's presidency.

David doesn't usually refer to his site as a blog, preferring the term *"Web portal."* He aims to provide his readers with valuable industry-related information. His readers are highly educated and value information, so it's important that the information presented is not trivial. Most of the information in David's posts comes from the FDA Web site. "Going to the FDA Web site is like visiting the Library of Congress," says David. "We sift through the information and present what is most relevant to our readers." Each of David's posts includes this valuable information and a link to an article or document on his Web site. "This drives traffic to the Web site where our training products and services are described and offered," explains David. "We also include a subtle ad in the form of an announcement for one of our products or services at the end of each posting." David's experience has been that readers are likely to purchase the products or services offered.

David started the blog in July of 2005, and in less than a year, he had more than 300 subscribers who all work for major corporations, his primary customers. He uses the free FeedBlitz service to allow visitors to subscribe and receive posts via e-mail. He gets new subscribers almost every day, and can tell from their e-mail addresses that they all are in his target market. This is in addition to readers who access the blog via feed readers like MyYahoo!, Pluck, or NewsGator, and who visit directly with their browsers.

David posts weekly or more frequently if he has timely information or an event to announce. David has lost only one subscriber since he started, and has seen an increase in product sales since starting the blog. To his knowledge, this is the only blog covering this topic, although there are a few Web sites that do.

Is the site working? Well, certainly a lot of people are reading it and sales are up. David is an astute businessman and usually has several initiatives under way, so it's hard to directly relate sales to any one initiative, but he feels that the Web portal is important to his business and he plans on continuing to provide valuable information to his readers.

36. CEO BLOGS

Top executives blogging

■ ■ ■

A CEO blog is "a blog written by a senior executive," says Debbie Weil, who writes about CEO blogs at BlogWrite for CEOs, *www.BlogWrite ForCEOS.com,* and is the author of *The Corporate Blogging Book.* "Could be a CXO or officer of a public company, but doesn't have to be. It's a convenient phrase that I was one of the first to use!"

"If the blogger is a clear thinker and cogent writer, a CEO blog definitely establishes them as an expert or thought leader in whatever their industry niche is," according to Debbie. Blogs can also give senior executives a direct conduit to rebut what they don't like in articles published about them in mainstream media.

CEO or senior exec blogs are still a new phenomenon. According to Jonathan Schwartz, COO of Sun Microsystems and a widely read blogger, blogs will become a must-have communications tool for every senior executive in a few years—just as e-mail is today. Debbie would like to believe that. "If communicating clearly—whether it's vision/goals/strategy—is the primary goal of a CEO, then a blog is the perfect bully pulpit, whether it's internal or external," adds Debbie.

"For senior executive bloggers, it's the voice and the writing style that seems to be a challenge," says Debbie. Many executives are not accustomed to writing in a personal and informal style. "Also, posting frequently enough can be a problem. For senior executives, once a week or even every ten days is fine. What to say doesn't seem to be so much a problem. They've got lots to say."

There can be disadvantages to CEO blogs as well. "For example, it can be a problem when there's lots of bad news in the mainstream press about your company, financial troubles, scandals, whatever, and you don't want to blog about it," says Debbie. "Well, you don't have to blog about it, but your readers may be expecting you to, once you've established a tone of transparency and authenticity in your blog."

And if you're a CEO, your blog is never just "personal." You represent the company you run, whether you intend to or not. Bob Parsons, founder of *GoDaddy.com,* wrote a series of blog postings about Guantánamo interrogation techniques that he later retracted. After retracting the posts, he wrote that he was "proud to say that GoDaddy is an American company." It's easy to imagine how Bob's personal sentiments might have been interpreted as statements about his company and its politics.

One popular CEO blogger is Alan Meckler, CEO of Jupitermedia. He's the principal shareholder and speaks freely in his blog. He sometimes blogs about behind-the-scenes details of acquisitions, revealing more about the financials behind the deal than you'd expect to get—and certainly more than you'd get in a press release. Mark Cuban, owner of the Dallas Mavericks, is another example of a CEO blogger who calls it as he sees it, misspellings and all.

There aren't many CEO blogs today, but the numbers are slowly increasing, and although there are potential disadvantages to having CEO blogs, for many senior executives, the positives far outweigh the negatives.

37. REAL ESTATE BLOGS

Real estate agents who blog have advantages

■ ■ ■

Paul Chaney, the vice president of Blogging Systems, is hot on real estate blogs. Although he admits that real estate blogs are in their infancy and that most real estate agents need a lot of education to get started blogging effectively, Paul lists a number of advantages for real estate agents who blog:

■ Blogs allow real estate agents and agencies to demonstrate their expertise by posting hints and tips about the real estate market as well as information about current events and trends. This expertise can go well beyond mere real estate, but also cover other information the real estate agent's target audience is interested in, such as community issues. Buyers are usually very interested in the community where a given piece of real estate is located, and real estate agents can demonstrate their knowledge of local issues and provide useful advice.

- Most of a real estate agent's business is built around his or her name. In many ways, real estate agents are their own brand. People like to deal with real estate agents they know and trust, especially because real estate is such an enormous investment. Because blogs are personal, readers can more easily come to feel that they know, and hopefully like and trust, the real estate agents, and want to do business with them.

- A blog can also make a real estate Web site come alive, sending it increased traffic because search engines favor blogs. Search engines drive most of the traffic on the Internet, and blogs are search engine–friendly by nature. Web sites are not search engine–friendly by default, and often need expensive expert tweaking to get substantial search engine traffic.

Paul also sees some real estate agents simply using blog software as a tool to post listings on the Internet easily, although this is not so popular. Although these sites may not fit some definitions of what a blog is, they provide a simple solution for getting real estate listings online, especially for nontechnical people.

Some great real estate agent blogs include much more than just listings. For example, one multiauthor blog focuses on Minnesota residential real estate. It has posts on closing costs and other fees in Minnesota, how much homes there cost, and local area information—lots of information useful for real estate buyers in Minnesota. It certainly helps establish the expertise of the two real estate agents blogging. It also features listings in the sidebars.

Some real estate blogs also are written for real estate agents. They generally are authored by organizations that sell products and services to real estate agents, such as training and software systems.

As with CEO blogs, some real estate agents who blog may encounter certain challenges. Like all marketing, blogging takes resources, especially time; busy real estate agents may find it difficult to make time to maintain a blog. Also, writing a blog is difficult for many real estate agents—they are often not accustomed to writing in such a personal style.

As real estate blogging matures, as more real estate agents blog, and as more collective experience is gained, these blogs will no doubt evolve, and effective techniques for reaching potential buyers and sellers will become better known.

38. LAWYER BLOGS

Word-of-mouth advertising on the Internet

■ ■ ■

Kevin O'Keefe is the president and founder of LexBlog, *www.lexblog.com,* which provides turnkey blog solutions for lawyers, allowing them to concentrate on publishing content in their areas of legal expertise. Kevin has 17 years of experience practicing law, so he has an inside perspective on the needs and wants of his clientele.

As Kevin told me, historically, lawyers have marketed themselves primarily through word of mouth. Referrals are incredibly important to both law firms and solo attorneys. Although some lawyers advertise, the practice is often regarded as distasteful, and many refuse to advertise at all. In fact, advertising for lawyers was illegal until the 1970s, distinguishing the legal profession from other professions and industries; most people still find their lawyers by word of mouth.

Blogs provide a way to extend "word of mouth" on the Internet and can be an invaluable tool for lawyers says Kevin. They help lawyers show their knowledge and passion for their work, and can also help them get the kind of work they prefer. Lawyers can identify their exact target audience and write material for them. Positive comments, as well as links and trackbacks, are referrals on the Internet. Although a single positive comment, link, or trackback may not have the same weight as a personal recommendation, most lawyers' blogs will accumulate many of these electronic recommendations, and also allow readers to see the lawyers' expertise firsthand.

Word of mouth and networking can go hand in hand. Lawyers may want to network more often, but it can be very difficult for them. Most lawyers are fairly busy and bill by the hour. Most networking opportunities take significant amounts of time. Blogging also takes time, but can be done whenever and wherever a lawyer has a few free moments, and blogs are relatively easy for lawyers to write for several reasons:

- Lawyers have to keep up-to-date with changes in the law, so the research that forms the basis of much of their blogging is already being conducted.

- Lawyers can leverage existing content. Many law firms produce newsletters and other material. This material often doesn't get as much visibility as it should, but placing it on a blog will give it widespread distribution.

- In Kevin's experience, it's really hard to get lawyers to write for newsletters, while, by comparison, most love to blog.

Lawyers do not have a great image. Let's be honest—even lawyers tell "lawyer jokes." Blogging can make lawyers seem more human, improving the public perception of their profession.

Kevin believes that eventually all lawyers will blog or otherwise publish via some personal publishing platform—the benefits are simply too great for them not to. The lawyers he sees blogging now are getting more work in the areas they enjoy. Whatever a lawyer's area of interest, blogging provides a great tool for professional networking and building clientele.

PART 3

PLANNING YOUR BLOG

■ ■ ■

Driving to work naked and starting a business blog with zero planning are similar. Both might start out OK, but will quickly go sour.

"Listen, I heard blogs are hot in the news, and our competitor XYZ Corporation has one. I don't know what a blog is, but start one. Today!"

No, no, no! A blog requires planning. The worst type of blog is the one started just for the sake of having a blog. Your blog needs to be part of your strategy, whether you are a mammoth multinational with a well-thought-out corporate communications and marketing strategy, or just one person like me, aka Demopoulos Associates.

What are the blog's main goals? Who will write it? What will it be about? Maybe you should simply encourage employees to blog instead of starting an official company blog? How will you keep the legal, marketing, and PR departments from turning your blog into a shiny and glossy highly produced site that lacks the personal feel and other advantages of a real blog? It takes planning, and the answers to these questions will vary with the size, structure, and culture of your company.

39.

BLOGS AND
THE BIG PICTURE

Begin at the end

■ ■ ■

"I always tell people to 'begin at the end,'" says Rick Short, director of marketing communications for Indium Corporation. What do you want to accomplish with your blog? "Close your eyes and imagine if everything you wanted to accomplish got done—what did you get done?" For example, if you're an expert on petunias and start blogging on petunias, do you want to become 'the go-to guy for petunias?'

"You're never going to get 'there' if there is no 'there,'" adds Rick. "Envision the best 'there' you can. What do you want—a Larry King interview? Women falling at your feet? What constitutes a 'home run'? That's how you should start."

Now that you know where you want to go, figure out where you currently are. List your strengths—reasons you've been successful so far. Fill in the dots as well as you can from where you are now to where you want to go. If you haven't blogged before, or aren't familiar with blogging, you might need to think of your journey in smaller steps.

"I started with a local fundraiser blog," says Rick. "But it didn't have legs—it was an annual event and not a year-round thing and it was boring." Although the blog itself wasn't a success, Rick learned a lot, both about blogging and his blog software. Rick suggests that novices consider "throwaway" blogs to gain experience. "You're going to learn things you can't even think to ask," says Rick. This can be a blog in an unrelated area that eventually gets deleted. He has commissioned throwaway blogs from some of his employees.

Rick also recommends reading as many blogs as possible and taking notes. What kind of blog is it? What are they trying to do? What do they want you to do? Does it seem effective?

Rick sometimes refers to the four Ps—four qualities that all successful business blogs need:

- *Point:* If your blog doesn't have a specific point (purpose), you will have a hard time attracting and keeping a readership.

- *Passion:* If you don't have a burning passion about the topic, why should anyone else be interested?

- *Personality:* If you don't have the personality for blogging, then find something else to do with your time. A blogger must be organized, enjoy researching blog posts, and like to present information.

- *Perseverance:* If you won't be able to stay with it once the blogging becomes routine, after you've battled with writer's block, after numerous distractions beckon, then you may not want to blog. "We're not talking about the first three months—it's about the 19th month and beyond," says Rick.

If you don't have any blogging goals, how will you achieve them? Once you have goals, you can plan how to get there. There may be many incremental steps, including learning how to blog well. You may want to start a "throwaway blog" before you start your permanent blog. Sometimes, planning is everything, and that certainly applies to blogs.

40. THREE KEY QUESTIONS TO ANSWER WHEN PLANNING YOUR BLOG

Planning is usually critical for success,
and blogs are no different

■ ■ ■

"When you start to put a business blog together, the planning phase is very important and ideally you should spend time working on these elements rather than diving straight in and writing your first post—as we all want to do!" says Mark White, e-marketing consultant and blogging specialist, of Better Business Blogging, *www.betterbusinessblogging.com,* based in London. "In this planning phase, you should identify what you hope to achieve with your blog and who you are writing for." This helps you focus your content and align it as closely as possible with the interests of your intended readers. Mark poses three questions:

1. "What is the blog looking to achieve?" Why do you want to start a business blog? "Are you looking to build a network of contacts for your company, or perhaps position yourself as an expert in your field, or promote a particular service or product using 'educational marketing,' or even help create a group of evangelists for your new product?" asks Mark. These are all perfect goals for a business blog, but you need to identify and focus on the primary goal to make it really successful.

2. "Who is the blog aimed at?" "You need to decide who is the target audience for your business blog, just as you do with your products or services," says Mark. This determines who you are writing for, and will help drive the content of your posts as well as the way you write them. The content and style of your blog will influence how your readers perceive you, so it's important to have a sense of what will appeal to them.

3. "What results are you looking for?" You should have some idea of what type of results you are trying to achieve. Many metrics are easily available, such as the number of visitors, subscribers to your RSS feed, sign-ups to a newsletter, contacts or clients initiated through a contact form on your blog, etc.

"Make sure that you spend time on this part of the setup of your business blog," says Mark. "If you do, you will reap the rewards because you will ensure that the blog maintains its focus in terms of its content and, as a consequence, provides your readers with what they are looking for."

41. THE WHO, HOW, WHAT, WHERE, AND WHEN OF BLOGGING

Don't blunder into blogging

■ ■ ■

"It's easy to blunder into blogging and then run dry of ideas and the blog peters out," says Richard Boyd of Oasis Design garden design and landscaping services, *www.realoasis.com.* Richard recommends you ask yourself the following questions before you begin: who, how, what, where, and when.

Who. "Find someone who is going to champion the blog," recommends Richard. Who is going to write the blog? You, someone else, a group of people? If you are in a larger organization, do you have support from above, or will you be doing it on your own time and initiative?

How. How will you be accessing your blog? Direct Internet access is common and ideal, and if you set up e-mail access as well, you can e-mail posts from almost anywhere.

What. "Decide upon your core blogging areas and try to rotate content on a regular basis," says Richard. Make sure you know whom your intended audience is and cater to them. "Use terminology . . . that they can easily grasp. Speak to them in their language, which may not necessarily be yours," suggests Richard.

Where. How does your blog fit in with the company Web site? The look and feel of the two need to marry up. "For us, our blog has become the FAQ, news, ideas, gossip, teaser, and extension to the company Web site," says Richard. "However, it took 6 + months for us to fully realize this and we are about to restructure the main Web site as a result." Richard also recommends that you create short items for the blog and feed these into in-depth articles within your Web site.

When. Update on a regular basis. "Your audience will get used to it and will look for your updates," says Richard. "Random and infrequent updates mean they tend to forget about your blog." You need to be committed to keeping your blog for the long run. Don't blurt out all your killer ideas at once. Write them down but don't publish them, and then you have a stockpile for those occasions when there is nothing happening.

"Give your blogging time," says Richard. It takes a while to build an audience. Study your log files: You may be surprised which posts generate the most interest and how people find your blog. Capitalize on this knowledge! Think of your blog as an extension of your Web site and generate a steady stream of valuable material.

42. FIVE-PLUS TIPS TO A BETTER BLOG

Great content plus Meryl's tips lead to a winning blog

■ ■ ■

"On a lark, I randomly surfed thousands of blogs covering many topics," says Meryl K. Evans. "It didn't take long to separate the good blogs from the 'could-be-betters.'"

Meryl is my favorite content maven, a whiz with words and more. She provides writing, editing, and copywriting services, and is not only a prolific writer but a prolific reader as well.

Meryl has boiled her blog observations down to five main recommendations:

1. "If you can't see the content without scrolling, then your banner is too big." No one comes to your blog to see the banner, the top fixed part of your blog that typically contains the blog title and description. Make sure your content is readily visible in the default window—Meryl recommends checking the site with your monitor set to 800×600–pixel resolution.

2. Write short posts. "Shoot for around 500 words or less," recommends Meryl. Although you may have an occasional longer post, "Save your longer stuff for newsletters and other more appropriate outlets. Readers want to get to the heart of the matter and get out."

3. Make sure your blog is readable and easy to look at. Skip the bright colors—"They ain't cool for serious blogs." Use italics sparingly. Font size is an issue as well. A reasonable font on your computer setup may appear quite differently on another. Check your font on multiple browsers and multiple computers if possible. Make sure your font can be changed with the browser's resizing feature, and you also might want to "offer two of three font options so all a user has to do is click on an option to make the font larger or smaller," suggests Meryl.

4. "If your blog isn't updated regularly, why should people come back to it?" asks Meryl. "They don't." Meryl suggests updating your blog at least two or three times a week.

5. "Arriving on a blog and getting greeted with music can freak out the reader, especially if he or she doesn't share the blogger's taste in music," says Meryl. Music is not standard, nor is it usually appreciated. Imagine a reader in an office or other public setting who may not want everyone around knowing what he or she is reading. Blogs should be silent.

A few extra suggestions from Meryl include: Have an "About" page; "choose a blog title or use a tagline that says what the blog is about"; "add a photo"—it helps humanize your blog"; "make your archives easy to find"; and "be accessible"—have an e-mail address or maybe even a phone number easily available.

Of course, content is important too! "If you have great content, the rest is easy. Just add the five tips," says Meryl. And if you "add the extras, then you're all set. If not, expect folks to click away within a blink of an eye after arriving on your blog. After all, it's a big blog world out there."

43. COMMON MISTAKES PROFESSIONALS MAKE WITH THEIR BLOGS

Watch out for these!

■ ■ ■

The Blog Squad says that "hundreds of blogs are started every day and many are abandoned. It's not enough to create a blog and post to it; you also need to use it effectively." The Blog Squad, Denise Wakeman and Patsi Krakoff, PsyD, are two well-known blog experts. "On a recent trip around the professional business blogosphere, we discovered several common mistakes professionals make with their blogs," add Denise and Patsi. They break these mistakes into two areas: content and design.

Content. For starters, many bloggers don't post often enough. Two or three times a week is a recommended minimum. And often the content isn't focused because the target audience isn't defined. You should know whom you are writing for.

Posts are often too long. Posts can be broken up with many blogging platforms' "extended post feature," which shows the beginning of a post and has a "click here to read more" or similar link. And posts should "link profusely." Linking to articles or other blog posts shows you've done your research and this helps the reader too.

Many blogs are full of simple errors and do not project a professional appearance. There is a difference between more formal business writing and blog writing, but that's no excuse for lots of misspelling and typos as well as poor grammar.

Design. Blogs are personal, and author information needs to be present, including a photo and a name, and for multiauthor blogs, some indication of who wrote individual posts.

Blogs should be interactive. Readers should be allowed to leave comments or at least interact in some way. And a blog should provide an easy way to subscribe, such as an RSS feed or an e-mail service like FeedBlitz. Several free e-mail add-ons are available that allow readers to subscribe and receive new blog posts via e-mail.

Random junk in the sidebar, including calendars, is popular with prime offenders. If content doesn't serve a purpose for the reader, it's just clutter; get rid of it.

Categories are a great way of allowing access to older posts and make much more sense than having only date-based archives, but some blogs don't provide categories, or simply have too many categories to make navigation useful and easy. Categories also enable your reader to find the content in which they are most interested.

The Blog Squad also has some quick comments on marketing mistakes. They include:

- Blogs often aren't submitted to blog directories: Blog directories are free. There is no reason not to submit. Especially for new blogs, directories such as *portal.eatonweb.com* and *www.globeofblogs.com* can help your blog get indexed by the search engines faster.

- Most bloggers don't ping, or send out a notification, each time a new post is published: Services such as *Pingoat.com* are free, fast, and easy to use, and alert Web log update services that your blog has been updated.

- Many blogs don't link to other blogs or use trackbacks, and have no blogroll, or list of other recommended blogs.

"A blog is like any other marketing tool —you've got to use it correctly to get positive results," according to the Blog Squad. They suggest making an effort to learn about your blogging software or hosting provider, and consider hiring a blog expert for help. Unfortunately, too many great Web sites are paired with a poorly done and amateurish blog! Personal and informal doesn't mean unprofessional, and a business blog needs to project a professional image.

44.

QUARTERLY
BLOG REVIEWS AND
EDITORIAL CALENDARS

Strategic blogging

■ ■ ■

"Many people think that if you just blog, good things will happen, such as new clients . . . flocking to purchase your services and products," says Michele Corey, cofounder of Advanced Approach, which offers consulting and coaching on personal and business growth strategies . Yes, that can happen, but Michele believes blogging should be strategic to help it succeed, especially as blogging continues to become more mainstream. You need to get the basics right and create a foundation.

Michele suggests a quarterly review to see if you are reaching your goals and attracting your target audience. Add your quarterly review dates to your calendar to help ensure they happen. Michele says, "A quarterly review will help you be a better blogger and help you really connect with what your readers most value." She recommends developing a set of questions that pertain to your goals and answering them at each review. "With a list of questions it's easy to review and notice trends over time," she adds. Her recommended questions are:

General.

- Is your blog strategy working? Are you gaining the results you wanted?

- How do you want to adjust your blog strategy (to meet your goals)?

- How many times per month did you blog over the past three months? Did you blog as often as you planned?

- Did you write your posts one at a time, or sit down and write one or two weeks' worth? What writing strategy works best for you?

Categories. Categories are simply subjects you write about. Most blogging software allows you to create and organize your blog posts by category, which helps both existing and new readers find your material via keywords in the search engines.

- Which categories were the most popular? (This is what your readers value and want to read about.)

- What do your readers comment about?

- Do you want to add, delete, or change your main category titles during the next quarter?

Statistics. You can learn a lot and help tune your blog strategy by looking at your Web site statistics. Your Web server or blogging platform may already have a good Web statistics platform built in, or a simple add-on such as SiteMeter or StatCounter can be used. You'll see how many readers you have, which posts are the most popular, what keywords and phrases people are typing into the search engines to find you, and much more. To help your readers find you in search engines, Michele recommends developing a list of keywords and using them in your blog posts and titles.

- Review your statistics:
    - What are your top three most read blog posts?
    - Which keywords and phrases are your readers targeting?
    - Do you want to add, delete, or change your keyword list?

Conclusions.

- What will you change?

- What will you keep doing more of to ensure the results you want?

- What would make blogging more enjoyable for you?

Most of her clients use her standard questions, but the more analytically inclined tweak the questions to better suit them and their business needs. If you've never conducted any kind of review of your blogging, you can expect some surprises!

Michele also recommends using an editorial calendar, which she calls the "Perfect Month Calendar." She describes it as "a simple outline that helps you beat writer's block and be more consistent with your blog posts." This could list what days you're planning on blogging, perhaps Monday, Wednesday, Friday, as well as what topics you wish to cover and keywords you intend on using. Of course, these should be topics that you have passion for, that your target audience is interested in, and that you are reviewing quarterly, right?

So what comes first, the editorial calendar or the blog review? It depends. Are you a beginning blogger? Start with an editorial calendar. Or if you're an established blogger, start with a blog review to help you establish what you want to stop doing and what you want to start doing more of until your next review, as well as create an editorial calendar to support your blogging choices.

You may choose not to be so structured and organized as Michele and her blogging clients, but some structure and planning can help almost any blogger.

45. PRACTICAL BLOGGING

Habits of highly effective bloggers

■ ■ ■

Robyn Tippins is a professional blogger. She has a personal blog, Practical Blogging, *www.sleepyblogger.com,* and also blogs for a number of other companies. Because she often blogs from early in the morning until late at night, she needs to be practical and effective.

"My number one blogging habit is definitely passion," says Robyn, echoing many other successful bloggers. Passion makes it easy, and your passion shines through in your writing.

"One of my favorite habits is blogging in the early morning," Robyn continues. She finds and blogs on a lot of information much earlier than the rest of the blogosphere, and, as a consequence, other bloggers are more likely to link to her. For a lot of people, blogging is like exercise; if they don't do it early in the morning, it never gets done.

Robyn suggests you read a lot of blogs, including smaller blogs that are not well known. Smaller bloggers put a lot of thought into what they write. She gets her best "scoops" from small blogs. Popular blogs find their scoops somewhere, and usually provide a link. "One of my favorite habits is to subscribe to those 'scoop' links when I see them," she says.

Robyn does quite a bit of preblogging preparation. She plans her blog post ideas and blog series. She especially likes to work on a blog series when news on a given topic is slow. She uses Google Calendar for planning, so she can pull the data from any computer with a browser.

Mobile blogging is important to Robyn, for she blogs all over the place. "I am very mobile and can take my computer anywhere so I am almost always online," says Robyn. Although she wouldn't recommend being so connected to everyone, she has an EVDO card for her laptop that gives her wireless access from almost anywhere, and a Palm Treo for mobile e-mail when she leaves the laptop behind. "I can literally be blogging riding down the road, waiting for my car to get serviced, or even sitting in a restaurant," she emphasizes.

"Going crazy with ads is the worst mistake bloggers can make," Robyn says. A blog that's all ads except the center column is overdone. "If a site has too many ads, they run the risk of scaring away readers . . . enough said," she adds.

Robyn stresses that networking is extremely important. "Link a lot, comment on other blogs, form collaborative projects, join e-mail lists, participate in the online conversation. . . . I would say this has been my most important habit."

Creating compelling, interesting, and useful content matters—a lot. "If your blog doesn't help people then they've no reason to come back," says Robyn. "Your content should be so good that they'll feel they can't miss a minute of it. Otherwise, you won't earn their viewership."

Some of these habits will be more valuable to you than others, depending on your blogging style and frequency, but bloggers at all levels can learn from Robyn. She truly is an effective and practical blogger.

46. HOW TO FIGURE OUT THE CONTENT DILEMMA

What am I going to write about?

■ ■ ■

"What? Me blog? What on earth would I write about?" are common thoughts from people who don't blog, and many bloggers themselves have difficulty with these questions. Tamera Kremer, founder of Wildfire Strategic Marketing, has a simple and sensible five-step process to help current and aspiring bloggers figure out the content dilemma.

1. What is your focus? You need to define your focus, instead of just writing about whatever interests you at the moment. What are you blogging about? Do you have a narrow focus or a wider focus? For example, are you writing about marketing in general or print advertising for the packaged goods industry? Tamera suggests "One hundred percent sticking to your subject."

2. What's on your list? What are you passionate about? What's on the list of what's important to you? This can help determine the direction your blogging takes. Tamera suggests you jot down notes as you think to help crystallize your focus.

3. Who's on your list? What other blogs are in your space? Any new sites or other online resources? You may want to blogroll and bookmark these online resources. How about offline resources that you read? Reading other people's thoughts, opinions, and experiences is an important part of blogging well and can help you determine what to write.

4. Who are you talking to? Who do you interact with in your daily life? Friends, colleagues, and customers can give you inspiration and ideas for your blog. They can spark interest or help set the direction you want to take certain posts in.

5. How to pull it all together, develop a plan, and be in for the long haul? This is the "How do I make sense of all this information?" step. Organization of content is as critical as the content itself. "You can have hundreds of links with no clue why you saved them," warns Tamera. Your links need to be annotated with why you thought they were worth saving. Some may be information you want to blog on, some may simply be interesting and spark additional thoughts, and some may be background material. If you've saved hundreds of links with no apparent reason why, most of them will end up being useless.

You also need to develop a blogging plan. How often will you blog? How much time will you spend? When are you going to do it? These are all things you need to think about. Tamera adds, "In order for blogging to work, it has to be integrated into your life."

You may not be able to sit down and answer all these questions immediately, but the exercise of trying will help refine your thinking and the focus of your blog, and help you find topics you're passionate about to blog on. Your answers may also change over time as your life, interests, and personal interactions evolve, and, of course, your blogging evolves.

47. DOES YOUR BLOG STINK?

Many business blogs could use some help

■ ■ ■

I spoke with Steve Remington at Why My Blog Stinks, *www.WhyMy BlogStinks.com,* on common mistakes many business bloggers make. Steve mentions his top five in no particular order.

Mistake one: not engaging in conversations. "This is where I think business blogs go wrong," says Steve. "If a business blog cannot engage in conversation, then there is no communication, and without communication, there is no 'community.'" Steve adds that a blog can have great content, but without conversation and community, it's merely a shadow of what it could be.

Engaging in conversations is as simple as answering comments. A blogger can answer comments in additional comments, or in a new post that addresses the comments. What, no comments enabled? With very few exceptions, Steve recommends you "open up those comments and get dialogue going."

Mistake two: fear of linking. You need to link to succeed, for a personal or especially for a business blog.

A blog with a lot of links is more valuable to the reader than a linkless blog; your links give readers more information about the topic at hand and establish your authority as a writer who is well informed about your subject.

Linking is also a great way to attract new readers; because most bloggers follow the referral links in their site statistics, they can see that you're linking to them and may pay a visit to your site. You'll be more likely to get valuable links from people you link with.

Mistake three: being long-winded. "One of the biggest mistakes bloggers make is posting extremely large articles," says Steve. It is great to have lots of content, but break it up and spread out your articles into several separate ones.

People on the Internet are in a rush. They tend to scan instead of read in detail. Make it easy on them. Emphasize each key point with its own post so they don't get lost! It's also easy to refer to your previous posts, as most bloggers often do, when they are short and to the point, instead of meandering through five-page monologues.

"What's the rush to say everything you know in less than two weeks?" asks Steve.

Mistake four: not posting regularly and consistently. When you post regularly and consistently, you'll have regular and consistent readers. "Keep that posting consistent and even, and make sure it is regular," recommends Steve. "Posting four or five times a month will cause you to lose readership and your blog will become stagnant."

Mistake five: not having a voice. Many business bloggers have a hard time taking a side and voicing their opinions. Often they see it as unprofessional, but there is a professional way to voice your opinions. "Bashing your opposition may not go over well, but sticking to your side of the issue and backing up what you have to say with facts is a professional way to do this," says Steve. "I honestly believe one of the largest mistakes business blogs make is trying to make everybody happy." You can't make everyone happy on controversial issues, so don't try. "Staying on middle ground is not a good way to go because in the long run you don't make anybody happy, you appear to have no backbone, and your voice is not legitimate," warns Steve.

Having an awareness of what your readers want, and how your blog looks to them, will help you develop a blog that stays current and is concise, well informed, and easy to read.

48. BLOGS AND PODCASTS IN THE ENTERPRISE

Be skeptical, be analytical, and move quickly

■ ■ ■

"Businesses should take a rational view of opportunities in social media," says Dennis McDonald, PhD, a management consultant. "Even if they decide against blogging, there may be other opportunities to engage with customers and vendors."

Dennis comes from a project-management and strategy-oriented IT management background, and says, "Web 2.0 has really struck my fancy, especially the move to more collaboration." Web 2.0 is a catchall phrase that refers to the new generation of interactive technologies and services available on the Web. Dennis now actively blogs and podcasts on business and consulting topics.

He's been researching how blogging and podcasting fit into IT services and corporate IT departments, including conducting an exploratory "Web 2.0 Management Survey" of how companies are managing Web 2.0 technologies such as blogs, podcasts, wikis, and social networking, available at *www.ddmcd.com/findings.*

Initially, he heard a lot of negative comments on how IT departments were firmly encamped in "the old guard" and resisting new technologies. His management survey showed that the issue is not just IT, but that many corporate cultures don't want to adopt the new openness and collaboration that social media encourages. Smaller and midsize companies are more likely to adopt social media, as their management structure tends to be less top-down and hierarchical, and they are more flexible and more likely to try new things.

Corporate culture is not the only reason why social networking technologies are not being adopted more rapidly. "It's shortsighted to say just 'corporate culture' is the issue," says Dennis. "There are also real financial concerns." Large organizations have major investments on their entire infrastructure of traditional and legacy technologies. They may still have nearly ancient mainframe computers and even older applications that still serve them well, so they can't just walk away.

Some will argue that a company can just embrace the new technology and start blogging. "The concept of 'free' corporate blogging is a myth," says Dennis. "Anyone blogging on corporate time is not doing something else. There is an opportunity cost." Doing it well, doing it right, requires management and realistic, commonsense policies. You can't just throw a switch and turn it on: The enterprise acceptance of Web 2.0 technologies, of social media, has cultural issues, financial issues, and technology support issues.

What does Dennis suggest? "Any large companies not looking at Web 2.0 technologies may be left in the dust by smaller competitors. You'd be insane not to look at them." Perhaps the best summary is Dennis's words, "Be skeptical, [be] analytical, and move quickly!"

PART 4

MAKING MONEY

■ ■ ■

Business is all about making money. Likewise, much of business blogging is directly or indirectly about making money—for example, by using blogs and podcasts to position yourself as a thought leader and expert and to promote your business.

Of course, it is also possible to explicitly make money from blogs and podcasts by running advertisements or selling products. Some business blogs and podcasts are even started specifically to generate profit as opposed to bolstering an existing business. Some professional bloggers report earning more than $100,000 yearly from their blogs, and, as we'll see in Part 7, some podcasts are bringing in serious money in the form of advertising and sponsorships.

Whether you choose to try and explicitly make money or not depends on your blogging goals as well as your thoughts and opinions. For example, plenty of bloggers run advertisements on blogs whose primary purpose is to bolster a preexisting business, while others wouldn't dream of running advertisements or other explicit money-generating schemes.

I ran advertisements for a while and didn't receive any negative comments from my readers. I decided, however, that the revenue was inconsequential in comparison to my consulting and speaking revenue, and removed the ads. Now the only things I advertise are my products that relate to my core business. It's up to you what you do, but remember that blogging is no get-rich-quick scheme.

49. CAN I MAKE MONEY BLOGGING?

It takes hard work and dedication

■ ■ ■

"The idea of sitting in your underpants writing about something you enjoy and making money at it certainly is an attractive one," says Chris Garret of Performancing, *www.performancing.com,* a group blog focused on making money from blogs. "Inevitably, though, people ask me if anyone can do it. My answer is a qualified 'Yes' . . ."

Most new businesses fail—many don't last a year. Similarly, most new bloggers give up within a year. Blogging is hard work. Most people are ready for the hard work the first few months, but what about 6 or 12 months out? "This can be particularly difficult if you have to hold down a job and family life at the same time," says Chris.

Also, money from blogging starts slowly. Significant money will come only months down the line after building traffic, reputation, and reader involvement steadily day by day. "When the rewards do start coming, they appear as a trickle, not a torrent," adds Chris.

Being a professional blogger involves more than just writing. You need to build traffic and get links. You can't assume that people will magically find your blog—you have to help them.

Sales is part of the job of a professional blogger. "Many of you will have read that *'sales'* word and shuddered. I feel the same way," says Chris. Unless you stick to Google AdSense or similar passive advertising, which is available to practically anyone who signs up, you'll need to sell! "That means sponsorships, advertiser relationships, affiliate schemes, and your own products," adds Chris. If you cannot sell and promote yourself, you are limiting your income potential. Yes, many people make a good deal of money out of AdSense, but AdSense and other passive ads do not perform well on all blogs—you may need to sell.

"You need something on offer over and above your blog posts," says Chris. A natural progression from content to product for many bloggers is to package their content and sell e-books, courses, or audio. Even if the same content is available spread through six months of blog posts, many people will pay for an updated and organized copy packaged as an e-book. Because e-books have zero distribution costs, they can be quite lucrative. In addition, you can write and distribute courses. Audio is also quite popular, both MP3s and CDs. One easy way to produce audio is to hold a teleseminar and record it. Free teleconferencing services are available, and you can let people listen for free or charge a modest fee. Some people have transcripts of their teleseminars created and sell them as additional products. "Think of what your readers might be interested in buying and find a way to provide it," recommends Chris.

Only a small percentage of people who attempt to make money from blogging succeed at actually making a living. Some professional bloggers make tens of thousands of dollars a year and a few actually make more than $100,000 annually. "Critical to success is having staying power, not being defeated by minor setbacks, being willing to put yourself out there, and put in the hard work," Chris emphasizes. "If you stick to it and can do all those things, then, yes, I am sure anyone can do it."

50. TIPS FOR ADSENSE AND OTHER ADVERTISEMENTS

Bigger advertising profits

■ ■ ■

"It costs your reader absolutely nothing to look at an ad on your site. It is a true win-win situation," says Reg Adkins, a behavior specialist, consultant, and counselor, who has experimented successfully with AdSense on his blog Elemental Truths, *elementaltruths.blogspot.com.*

AdSense advertisements from Google are almost ubiquitous on Web sites and are probably the most popular advertising for blogs. Almost anyone can sign up and once approved can easily add AdSense ads. AdSense is a "pay per click" advertising scheme—you get anywhere from a few cents to a few dollars every time someone clicks on an ad.

What is the right mix when tweaking your site to achieve the right balance of content, design, and commercialism? "That depends on you," says Reg. Some people prefer to have no advertisements on their blogs, while others have blogs specifically to host advertisements, and many people fall in between. Also, if you restrict your advertising to one or two items, your click-through rate per advertisement will increase.

Continuity between ads and content is very important. "If your advertisement looks like your article, your click-through rate will increase," says Reg. He recommends removing the outline boxes from your ads, for they set the ads apart and cut down on the flow. Matching the background color of the ad to that of your site, and the color of the ad text to the color of the text on your site, adds to the continuity of the site also. Having your advertisements in the body of your posts is another way to increase your click-through rate, for your visitors are more likely to click through if they do not have to scroll around to get to the advertisement. You want your ads to look like part of the site—not set apart as obvious and glaring advertisements.

Relevant ads receive more clicks. If your advertisement is related to the content of your article, your click-through rate will increase. AdSense ads are contextual—the ads displayed depend on Web site content. "To get relevant AdSense ads, try to use keywords in the title of your article and intersperse them through the first couple of paragraphs," recommends Reg.

Reg also suggests, "Be very careful before adding the big commercial ads to your site. Unless you are talking specifically about products they offer, you won't make much profit there." Ads for specific products need to be related to your blogging topics to succeed. AdSense automatically displays ads related to your content, but other types of advertisements typically do not.

Reg has found that a few simple tweaks to your ads can greatly improve profitability. The key is to experiment and find what works best on your site, and these suggestions are a great place to start!

51. E-COMMERCE AND BLOGS

E-commerce sites that add blogs
report increased sales

■ ■ ■

Higher Web site traffic and increased sales—that's what Jeremy Bloom has gotten every time he's started a blog for his e-commerce clients, a couple dozen in just the past few months. Jeremy is an e-commerce expert and consultant and a founder of Techvertising, *www.techvertising.com,* and knows that blogs are an enormous step forward.

Jeremy likens the emergence of the blogosphere to the invention of the printing press in impact. The printing press changed books forever—suddenly they could be published instead of painstakingly, slowly, and expensively copied by hand. An ordinary person could not have practically owned a book previously. The printing press made books accessible to ordinary people—at least once they learned to read!

Similarly, with blogs, anyone can publish. The spread of the Internet was a big step—everyone could theoretically have a Web site—but blogs make it possible for almost anyone to publish on the Internet because blogging software makes a knowledge of Web design and coding unnecessary. The average person or even small business usually doesn't know how to use Web site authoring software. They may hire someone, and then end up with a somewhat static Web site that they can't easy update or add material to.

"Every company seems to have a Web site nowadays, but trying to get attention via your typical business Web site is like trying to get attention by holding up an 8½ × 11–inch sign in Times Square," says Jeremy. "The key to a successful Web site is content." It's often said that "Content is king," and this is absolutely true. If a Web site has good content, and plenty of it, visitors may have a reason to stay around and come back later. The more time they spend on the site, the more likely it is they'll spend money.

People need to find your Web site first, and blogs are almost search engine optimization (SEO) magic. Search engines favor sites with frequently updated content, and blogs make creating and publishing content easy. However, Jeremy often sees companies wasting far too much time and effort on SEO, instead of concentrating on more important e-commerce issues such as building e-mail lists and ease of use. Although some basic Web site SEO is important, most e-commerce companies should concentrate in more critical areas as well as start blogging.

Jeremy recommends different uses of blogs for his e-commerce clients depending on their needs and the maturity of their Web sites. Sometimes he starts a traditional blog for a company and gets them blogging—hopefully producing great content and attracting increased Web site traffic. Other times he'll simply use the blogging software to put existing content, such as customer newsletters or press releases, on the Web. He loves WordPress for its flexibility—the result doesn't need to look like a blog, and he rarely even mentions the word *"blog"* to his customers in this case. Sometimes he'll scrap existing customer Web sites entirely and replace them with a blog. Because WordPress offers the flexibility to create static pages—essentially ordinary Web site pages—he can use it to create a standard-looking Web site as well as a traditional blog if desired.

It's all about content. Blogs and blogging software make it easy to publish content for almost anyone. The more content, the more visitors, and for e-commerce sites, that translates to more sales.

52.

SHOPPING CARTS
FOR BLOGS
(AND OTHER WEB SITES)

Shopping carts that help sell

■ ■ ■

"Would you like fries with that?" asks Tom Antion, referring to the ability of a shopping cart to suggest related products to someone ordering, perhaps with a package discount. "This is real power and something you absolutely want in a shopping-cart system," says Tom, a well-known Internet marketing guru and professional speaker. After all, the buyer already has his or her credit card out and has decided to buy—this ability to "upsize" can add enormously to sales and profit.

An electronic shopping cart operates with a physical shopping cart metaphor. Shoppers add items to electronic shopping carts as they shop, and "check out" when they are ready to pay, usually with a credit card. Items for sale on a blog often appear on the sidebars and occasionally in the posts. Clicking on an item usually brings you another page that has more information on the product, which may be located on a related Web site or electronic storefront.

Literally thousands of shopping-cart systems are available for little or no cost. "Basically, they just take the order like a cashier," says Tom. "They don't do anything to help you sell. Picking a shopping cart is a very serious decision you will likely have to live with for a long time."

It's also possible to have a shopping cart custom built. Tom strongly recommends against this approach. "You better be prepared for some frustration and delays making it all work. Believe me, I know." Tom had his first shopping cart custom built, for many commercial options weren't available then, and "I'll never do it again," insists Tom. "It was a total nightmare!"

Tom recommends smart shopping-cart systems that automate as much as possible—with functions such as calculating shipping and taxes and capturing customer data, including e-mail addresses—as opposed to a simple cart with limited functionality. Smart shopping systems "will dramatically increase sales because they manage the entire shopping experience, including upselling the customer, making and handling special offers," and much more, says Tom.

According to Tom, some features to look for in a shopping-cart system include:

- Upsizing capability—a cart that will help you sell additional products during a sale

- Shipping and tax calculations—some carts do this better than others

- Soft and hard goods—the capability to sell both digital downloads, such as e-books and audio files, as well as traditional "hard" merchandise

- Associate program capabilities—an associate program lets others promote your products via a link, and automatically calculates and tracks commissions when sales occur. "This basic premise made *Amazon.com* a billion-dollar company," says Tom, and it's "like having an army of commissioned salespeople working for you."

- Coupons and discount capabilities—which can "mean a tremendous boost in sales"

- E-mail integration—a great shopping cart will send a confirmation e-mail when a sale is completed, keep a database of e-mail addresses, and allow you to broadcast to whatever subset of customers you'd like, and much more.

For years, Tom didn't recommend or endorse a specific shopping cart because none of them had all the functionality he required. However, Tom now has a favorite cart he recommends—he likes it so much he has licensed it and rebranded it as *www.KickStartCart.com.* Whether you chose Kick-StartCart or another shopping cart, remember that you'll probably live with your choice for a long time. You might not need some of the features Tom mentions today, especially if you start out selling only one or two products, but features such as upselling, coupon capability, and associate programs can mean substantial revenue in the long run.

53. CREATING AND SELLING INFORMATION PRODUCTS FROM YOUR BLOG

Blogging is all about information

■ ■ ■

"Wouldn't you love to have your own product to sell?" says Brian Clark, better known as the copyblogger, *www.copyblogger.com.* Blogs are great for both creating and selling information products, according to

Brian. Information products contain knowledge in an easily digestible format, for example e-books and how-to videos. You could sell someone else's information products though various affiliate programs, but Brian suggests you create your own. "It puts you in the best position in the online sales world," stresses Brian.

"I believe it's important that you have a great deal of either knowledge or passion about any topic that you develop into an information product," says Brian. Knowledge makes it easy, but passion lets you approach the topic without any preconceptions and a fresh perspective. There may be a steep learning curve, but passion helps carry you through it happily.

"Once you've got a general topic, start blogging," recommends Brian. "You don't necessarily need or even want to know exactly what your product will be." Readers' comments and questions and the popularity of posts will help you determine what direction to go, and you can even survey readers to find out what they're interested in. "The secret to hitting a home run with an information product is to *ask* your readers what they want," says Brian.

If your product is a book or e-book, you can blog it. Or your posts might become the basis for an audio product sold as a CD and perhaps a downloadable MP3 or even video. Your reader interaction can help with fine-tuning to create an information product people are really interested in.

What? Why would anyone buy something that you've essentially published for free online? "Due to the reverse-chronological order of blog posts, it's a really bad way to digest large chunks of information," says Brian. "Having the same information in book, audio, or video format is much easier to deal with." He also points out, "The key is getting the product finished" and making your best efforts available, rather than spending too much time trying to make it perfect.

You can also offer a chapter or two, or perhaps a part of an audio series, for free. "This is a tried-and-true method," says Brian. Require readers to give you an opt-in e-mail address in exchange, so you can follow up with reminders, special offers, and more.

Brian suggests, "You can also *tell and sell* via a minicourse or tutorial that explains what the content is all about, as well as highlighting the benefits of having access to it." Your complimentary tutorial should be in the same format, with hints at what the full learning experience will be like after purchase.

"No matter what preselling technique you use, you'll still need a sales page that entices people to click through and order," stresses Brian. It needs to have a great headline, restate the core benefits of your product, and follow those up with the features that support your benefits. "The idea is for your blog combined with your excerpt or tutorial to have presold the reader, so that they simply scan your sales page and order. It's important to have a substantive, low-hype sales page, with plenty of those testimonials that you acquired from key people in your niche and from select subscribers. A money-back guarantee also helps boost sales immensely," suggests Brian.

"There's no better business in the world than being both the manufacturer and direct seller of your own high-margin product," says Brian. Information products are great, for it takes only your mind and time to create them, and some smart blogging to sell them.

54. ANDRE, THE SPLOGGER

How spam bloggers operate

■ ■ ■

"Many sploggers are scum, but I'm not," insisted Andre as he slammed the table in front of us, rattling the vodka bottle. "Most of us are not criminals or opportunists, just honest businessmen. A few criminals in our midst try to brand us all as evil!"

A *splog* is a "spam blog." Although many debate the exact definition, *Wikipedia.org* describes a splog as a blog that

> the author uses only for promoting affiliated web sites. The purpose is to increase the PageRank of the affiliated sites, get ad impressions from visitors, and/or use the blog as a link outlet to get new sites indexed. Content is often nonsense or text stolen from other web sites with an unusually high number of links to sites associated with the splog creator which are often disreputable or otherwise useless web sites.

Spam blogs are serious problems on free blog sites such as *Blogger.com,* and spam blogs often clog search results, making it more difficult for potential readers to get to blogs with real content. Spam in all its embodiments is the bane of the Internet.

I met Andre in the Hotel Taroy bar in Khanty-Mansiysk, Central Siberia. I stopped by for a beer and we started chatting at the bar. "I am a cab driver, reindeer breeder, and Internet entrepreneur," he claimed as he introduced himself. I figured he probably ran a few Google AdSense ads on his reindeer breeder Web site. It quickly became clear he was a splogger.

Andre categorizes splogs into three rough categories:

1. Blogs that have nonsense text, but the right keywords and right keyword density to attract good search engine rankings. He considers these "immoral."

2. Abandoned blogs that have been hijacked. Many bloggers eventually give up, and their blog URLs may have some value: links from other blogs, occasional visitors, and search engine traffic. Andre describes sploggers who do this as "clearly criminal and thieves."

3. Blogs that have useful information, but nothing unique. These blogs usually take their content from other Web sites.

Andre's blogs fall into the later category. They have useful content, but it's all copied from elsewhere. Andre says that many sploggers steal their content from other Web sites, although he uses another popular approach: He usually gets content from free article directories such as *ezinearti cles.com* and *goarticles.com.* He says he would never steal material—why, when so much free material is available?

He was somewhat vague when it came to how he made money from splogs, but he said that it required constant experimentation and adjustments. Last year's winning techniques, sometimes even last month's, often don't work well anymore. He uses a combination of advertisements, affiliate links, and linking strategies to make money and drive traffic to his other sites. The details are "trade secrets," he claimed several times. The number of splogs he has and creates are also a secret, but "more is not always better—it's not like vodka," Andre laughed.

Andre uses automated tools to create the majority of his splogs. He also sometimes employs cheap labor, both from home and abroad, to defeat CAPTCHAs, those "annoying 'type in the characters from the picture above'" designed to stop automated tools.

Andre is a self-described Internet entrepreneur. Splogs are "just one tool in [his] bag of tricks," and they are becoming less effective, "just as e-mail doesn't work as well as it used to." Andre claims to hate spam—he says he would never use e-mail spam, comment spam, or trackback spam. His splogs do contain useful information, not junk text. His advice for wanna-be Internet entrepreneurs: "Keep testing new techniques and always deliver value to your customer." Interesting words for a splogger!

55. BLOG NETWORKS

Power in numbers

■ ■ ■

Interest in blog networks has increased, and they have been sprouting up like weeds, especially since AOL's multimillion-dollar purchase of Weblogs, Inc., a pioneering blog network.

Paul Short of *Bloglogic.net,* a small innovative blog network, defines a blog network as just a series of blogs on different topics or in a vertical market. The blogs can be owned by one parent company or loosely tied together in some other way.

Paul sees two main advantages to blog networks:

1. Blog networks can funnel traffic between sites. They do this in a number of different ways, including by linking within posts to other blogs in the network, linking from the sidebars, or posting summaries of popular posts on all the blogs in the network.

2. Blog networks attract advertisers, for the number of combined page views across the network can be very significant. A blog that receives 500 page views a day is not very interesting to most big

advertisers, but a blog network with 100 such blogs is receiving 50,000 page views a day. That is a significant number that can attract advertisers.

Paul says there are different ways to look at and categorize blog networks. Some blog networks offer magazine-style blogs, such as Gawker Media's popular Lifehacker blog at *www.lifehacker.com*. It has multiple authors, pumps out lots of material daily, and resembles a magazine more closely than a typical solo-author blog. Other blog networks contain a number of blogs in very specialized areas. An example would be b5media, and their array of niche blogs in areas like Hilary Duff news, *www.hilarynews.com,* Asian food, *www.noodlesandrice.com,* and MTV, *www.mtvrealityworld.com.*

Another way to look at blog networks is by ownership. Some blog networks, such as Gawker Media, own all their blogs and often hire writers for specific blogs. Others range from independent blogs whose owners have banded together to hybrid models such as b5media where some blogs are owned and some are independent.

Paul sees a lot of weak blogs that wouldn't succeed on their own fortified by blog networks. Blog networks typically have extremely popular anchor sites, and other less popular blogs that get the majority of their traffic from the anchor sites. Very often there is zero promotion other than this shuffling of traffic.

In the future, Paul would like to see blog networks where each blog is independently valued and promoted. He also sees more "community features" coming from blog networks as they mature and grow. Examples of community features might include a multimedia newsletter that includes content from across the network, including audio and video. Another great idea is a forum where visitors can interact—some way for them to communicate between themselves, other than by leaving comments on specific blogs on specific posts. This feature can get visitors to actually generate content, instead of merely commenting on content, and can lead to a more vibrant blog network community.

Blog networks, just like blogs, are new and evolving. As the blogosphere expands, we can expect changes in the form, content, and networking and communication opportunities it offers.

56. BLOGGING FOR A BLOG NETWORK

How is it different?

■ ■ ■

Blogging for a blog network is different than blogging on your own. You need to be disciplined. You must stay focused on your topic. You need to keep posting regularly. These could be described as benefits or restrictions, depending on your outlook, but there are some undebatable advantages to this style of blogging.

Three major benefits are that you belong to a network of professionals, you gain immediate recognition as a professional writer, and you usually get paid, according to Bill Belew, who blogs for the Know More Media blog network, primarily on Asian business. Sure, some bloggers will claim that you can achieve all three without writing for a blog network, but a blog network makes them automatic.

As soon as Bill joined the Know More Media network, he was immediately connected with about 70 other staff bloggers. He could share war stories, victories, and techniques. He had other people to compare statistics with, such as the number of visitors and page views. For example, Bill wrote a blog series—a series of connected blog posts that appeared over a period of time. It generated a lot of traffic, and he promptly shared that technique with other Know More Media bloggers, who used it successfully.

Bloggers get paid for writing when they belong to a blog network. A solitary blogger can attempt to monetize his or her blog by adding Google AdSense ads, for example, but many great bloggers barely make enough money to buy a cup of coffee a week. In contrast, although Bill isn't going to get rich, "It pays my mortgage." Bill also works as a teacher for the University of Phoenix, so blogging is not his sole source of income.

Bill is recognized as a professional writer, because he gets paid. Yes, some solo bloggers have managed to get press credentials occasionally, even to events such as the Republican and Democratic national conventions, but it's certainly the exception, not the rule. Bill regularly gets press credentials and attends events that would otherwise be closed to him or expensive to attend. "It opens doors that don't normally get opened up," says Bill.

When I spoke to Bill, he had seen two U.S. secretaries of state and Steve Ballmer from Microsoft speak in the past two weeks, had attended the annual conference of the Committee of 100 (a membership organization composed of Chinese-American leaders), and had been to several other important events recently. He not only has a great time and gets to question dignitaries and leaders, but he finds lots of great content for his blogging, content that cannot be found on the Internet!

Immediate press credentials and recognition as a professional writer, a network of like-minded people for support and bouncing ideas around, and money—joining a blog network can be a great opportunity for bloggers who are knowledgeable, committed, and interested in working as part of a team.

57. PASSION, PERSISTENCE, AND PROFIT

Boston Sports Media Watch

■ ■ ■

Every day from 6 to 8 AM, Bruce Allen reads the sports sections of 15 newspapers online, checks other online sources including blogs, and posts summaries, links, and commentary to his Boston Sports Media Watch blog, *www.bostonsportsmedia.com*. He loves doing it and would do it for free, although he is elated to be making money. He spends about four hours a day on his blog, including answering e-mails. A few thousand sports fans check his site at the beginning of the workday, including his boss at his day job in IT.

Boston Sports Media Watch grew out of Bruce's lifelong love of sports. He found media coverage of many sporting events somewhat biased. "Some [media outlets] are more biased than others, and some really annoyed me," says Bruce. He also wanted to collect as much sports information on Boston area sports teams in one place as possible.

Bruce started in April of 2002 with a free *Blogger.com* account and a lot of passion. He found building a Web site overwhelming, despite being a computer guy, but creating a blog was simple. Three months later, Bill Griffith, a sports writer for *The Boston Globe,* mentioned Boston Sports Media Watch in a column, and traffic started to explode. Bruce has since upgraded to Movable Type blog software and his own domain; he gets 5,000 to 6,000 unique readers a day, 100,000 a month, and about 2,000,000 page views a year.

Bruce makes money from his site with a mixture of Google AdSense ads, *Blogads.com* ads, and some Amazon affiliate links. "It's definitely worth my time," says Bruce. "It's a great side income." In a good month, Bruce makes the equivalent of about one-third to one-half of his monthly salary from his site. Google AdSense and Blogads bring in roughly equal revenue, with Amazon a distant third.

Bruce is reluctant to take on the title of "media"—although he certainly is part of the media. "I know I have influence," he says, but the rules are different for bloggers than for mainstream media. He has more flexibility and freedom, and tries hard to provide comprehensive and fair coverage.

Boston Sports Media has had steady traffic for the past two years, but it hasn't been increasing. Bruce would like to take it to the next level, but he realizes he'll probably never entirely support himself from his site. In the meantime, Bruce is engrossed in his passion for sports, and making a great side income, with fringe benefits such as free copies of new sports books and invitations to sporting-related events.

PART 5

PROMOTING YOUR BLOG
AND TRACKING STATISTICS

■ ■ ■

"Write it and they will come generally doesn't work well." Yes, if Mick Jagger, the Pope, or Osama bin Laden start blogging, they'd probably have a lot of readers very quickly, but even they would need some publicity! And you and I are neither that famous nor that notorious. Promoting your blog—driving or enticing readers to your blog—is part of blogging. Many bloggers enjoy promoting their blogs, for many social aspects are involved; blogging is about conversations, and conversations are inherently social.

Promoting your blog and building readership is generally a slow uphill climb. But slow uphill climbs can be pleasurable; just ask world-famous bicyclist Lance Armstrong. Of course, everyone has his or her own idea of slow.

How do you know if your blog is succeeding? There are several ways, and not all require lots of visitors. All things being equal, however, more visitors are better than fewer. Tracking your visitors via Web statistics is one way to measure success, and this information can be very powerful. Is one post or type of post far more successful than others? Maybe you should concentrate on more posts like that. Where are your readers coming from? Maybe they come from an e-mail subscription using a free interface such as FeedBlitz (discussed on page 114), maybe they are following a specific link with their browser, or maybe they have subscribed via your site feed. Again, this can be valuable information. Knowing as much as you can about your readers is valuable—after all, one of your goals is to please them and keep them coming back.

58. GREAT BLOGGERS ARE GREAT CONVERSATIONALISTS

Listening well is an important skill

■ ■ ■

"Blogs are about conversations, and the best bloggers tend to be the great conversationalists," says Stephen Turcotte, the president and founder of Backbone Media, one of the first Internet firms to specialize in search engine positioning. He has a track record of successfully spotting online trends that are going to become important. He is firmly on the blog band-wagon and believes the blog party has just begun. He's working on a service named Scout, *www.scoutblogging.com,* to make bloggers better conversationalists by helping them listen more effectively.

Stephen believes the best conversationalists are always those who listen well. The hardest part for most of us is listening, not talking. As this idea translates to the blogosphere, it's easier to post than to keep up with what the other bloggers in your topic area are saying.

Listening, Stephen believes, involves finding and reading a lot of blogs in your area of interest, the area you blog about. Stephen likes to compare it to a gigantic searchable cocktail party. Blog search engines can be an enormous help in finding like-minded blogs, as can be the blogrolls of blogs in your area you've already identified.

Feed readers can also help enormously once you've determined which blogs you want to follow, but the blogosphere is dynamic, and you had better expect your "must-read" blog list to grow and evolve. Keeping up is hard to do!

Let's say you're a dog blogger—perhaps a veterinarian blogging on dog health issues. You can find other interesting dog blogs by using the blog search engines, as well as by following blogrolls, trackbacks, and comments on those blogs. You'll learn what others are saying in the dogosphere, the part of the blogosphere focused on dogs (OK, I just made that up!). Monitoring del.icio.us, a social bookmarking site, is another way to find relevant content that other people are linking to. By noting which dog posts have the most comments and trackbacks, as well as which topics have the most posts, you'll get a good idea of what dog blog readers are particularly interested in. In your real-world life, as a veterinarian, you'll also have a new resource for valuable information on both health issues dog aficionados are interested in and others they should be interested in—real-world information shouldn't be discounted at all, and tends to mirror online information eventually.

So what should this veterinarian do if she wants to become a popular dog blogger? Well, Stephen believes she needs to spend a lot of time reading and interacting with other dog blogs and bloggers. As a seemingly infinite amount of time can be spent surfing the blogosphere, this might appear to be an onerous task! Look for opportunities to add value to a conversation. Veterinarians, just like all of us, are pretty busy people. This veterinarian is probably passionate about dogs—why else blog about them? She probably loves reading about dogs, and although a lot of time may be involved, she probably doesn't consider it work!

The best bloggers do more than blog. They spend significant time reading other blogs and otherwise interacting in the blogosphere.

59. EVANGELIZING YOUR BLOG

Guy Kawasaki on blog popularity

■ ■ ■

"Welcome to my first attempt at blogging," wrote Guy Kawasaki in late December of 2005. "Admittedly, I'm three years behind the bleeding edge, but I had to get over the inherent arrogance of blogging: that people would give a shiitake about what I have to say." Guy, an author, columnist for *Forbes.com,* managing director of Garage Technology Ventures, one of the original Apple Computer employees responsible for the marketing of the Macintosh, and a blogger who is well known for bringing the concept of evangelism to high-technology businesses, has learned that people are indeed interested in what he has to say. He's successfully evangelizing his blog, just as he previously evangelized the Apple Macintosh and his books.

"Think of your blog as a product," says Guy. If you want people to read it, you want as good a product as possible. Every time you're writing a post, think about whether anyone will care. If no one will care, you've got a poor product. You need to create great content people care about. "It's tough to market crap," he adds, and suggests that you "market the heck" out of your blog. He also suggests that you think of your blog as a book instead of a diary. Diaries, unlike books, are written with no expectation that anyone else will read them.

Guy recommends that you e-mail people when you start your blog. "When I started my blog, I sent out 10,000 e-mails," he says. However, he warns against spamming—don't e-mail people who haven't e-mailed you. When he replies to e-mails, he also includes a "by the way I'm blogging now" message, and includes his blog address in his e-mail signature.

So, how do you let others who blog on similar topics know about your blog? First you blogroll: find blogs on similar and related topics and add links to them from the sidebar of your blog. Most bloggers will notice a new link to them and will check out your blog. "You never know what they might do for you," says Guy.

Getting links to your blog is important. People follow links, and links cause the search engines to rank you more highly and send you more traffic. One way is to find interesting yet obscure topics and blog on them. Others who link to what you've uncovered will tend to link to you, too. Also, if you find a popular blogger who has written on a topic you know about extensively, write a follow-up and let that blogger know—maybe he or she will link. Guy loves it when people do this and he enthusiastically links to them.

Commenters are your friends, even if they don't always agree with you. "Only good things can happen when you read all the comments in your blog and respond to them. It makes commenters return to your blog," says Guy. Most of us receive just a few comments. Maybe one in a hundred visitors, maybe fewer, leave a comment. Make readers who take the time to comment feel special and valued, because they are.

Although you are trying to create a great product, don't be afraid to speak your mind! "If you can't speak your mind on your own blog, we might as well all give up and stay on the porch," says Guy. People value honest opinions in the blogosphere, whether they agree with them or not.

Guy considers his blog a product, similar to his books. He's been relentless in marketing it and in his quest to climb the Technorati 100—a list of the 100 most popular blogs (he's at number 32 right now). You may not be as shameless an evangelist as Guy; you probably don't have as many e-mail addresses and haven't written eight books. But Guy still feels that evangelizing your blog—marketing and promoting it because it's great—is the way to get more readers. If you don't think it's great, why should anyone else? And if it's great, shouldn't you tell everyone?

60. SEARCH ENGINE OPTIMIZATION FOR BLOGS

Linking and keyword strategies

■ ■ ■

"The goals of the search engines are to mimic humans, so if you write information that humans like, the search engines will eventually like it too," says Aaron Wall, SEO guru and author of the well-regarded *SEO Book* and SEO Book blog, *www.seobook.com.* Most Internet traffic is driven by search engines, and search engine optimization (SEO) means developing Web pages and sites, including blogs, to maximize the number of visitors sent by the search engines.

Search engine strategies include linking strategies and keyword strategies. "Each link is seen as a vote to the search engines," says Aaron, "although not all links are considered equal." Links from more popular sites are more important, as are links that contain descriptive text. Keywords and phrases are terms users type into search engines to find content, and using popular and appropriate keywords within your blog posts is important too.

Search engine optimization strategies for blogs depend on the type of blog you have. "If there is lots of competition in your topic area, you might need to optimize for social interaction in order to get links." For example, there are many computer technology blogs, so social interaction and the resulting links are extremely important. In less saturated areas you can concentrate on keywords and phrases.

How do you work on getting links? Simply via social interaction. Surf around for interesting things in your area and leave comments. If you do, people are more likely to read what you write and hopefully link to it. "Don't leave cheesy comments," warns Aaron. "The goal of comments is to stick out and be useful and remarkable."

You should also link out extensively in your own posts for many bloggers will notice if you link to them. "For a new blogger, linking out to other related blogs and quality content is the cheapest form of marketing possible," according to Aaron. You can also link to your own posts from other posts, using good, descriptive link text whenever possible. For example, instead of a link saying, "As I said *here* in regard to my library visit," it's better to write, "When I commented on *finding marriage records at the Los Angeles Public Library.*"

Although relevant content is important, Aaron also concedes that "sometimes just a rant that draws attention is good." Controversial posts can be especially good at getting attention and links. Sometimes you can even predict which people or groups may be most likely to notice, link, and comment.

Choosing good keywords is important, especially in less saturated subject areas. Several keyword research tools are available, but Aaron thinks the Google Keyword research tool, currently at *adwords.google.com/ select/KeywordToolExternal,* is "the only keyword tool anyone needs." For example, if you're blogging on "baldness remedies," you may want to know that "baldness cures" is searched on more frequently and modify your text appropriately.

The most important place to have keywords is in the title. People also often use the post title text for links, giving you valuable links with keywords in the link text.

Try to stay on topic within a post. If your post meanders, others are less likely to link to it, and it's also harder to link to yourself intelligently. In general, fewer words are better than more words. If you must write long posts, try to write the authoritative document on your topic so that others are more likely to link to you rather than duplicating your efforts. It's also important to use categories with appropriate keywords, which almost all modern blogging software supports; this will make it much easier for visitors to navigate your site and find the content they want.

Regardless of what type of blog you write and whether it's in a competitive area or not, it's important to write informative posts. An occasional controversial post can be good, too. Don't pay too much attention to keywords—if every post is optimized for keywords, the blog can seem unnatural. Remember that search engines aim to emulate humans, so write your blog with the goal of making humans like it!

61. THE BLOG TRAFFIC KING ON BUILDING BLOG TRAFFIC

The key to traffic is offering valuable content

■ ■ ■

"An established blogger probably cares about one thing and one thing only—how to increase traffic," says Yaro Starak, "Blog Traffic King." "This is the core concern for most bloggers. You need people to read what you write and hear what you say. The more people you can get to, the better!"

The key to traffic is offering valuable content, according to Yaro. Writing valuable content and attracting more traffic is not complicated, but it can be time-consuming and laborious. Yaro spent the last six months of 2005 working to increase the traffic to his primary blog, Entrepreneur's Journey, *www.entrepreneurs-journey.com,* from 0 to 1,000 daily visitors— quite a feat! He then rightfully crowned himself Blog Traffic King, started a free newsletter covering different aspects of growing traffic to blogs, and is starting a Blog Traffic School.

Yaro has a concept he calls "pillar articles." Pillar articles are at the heart of every popular blog. A pillar article consists of timeless information, not news or personal blogging, and is relevant to a wide audience for a long period of time. It might provide a definition of a key term, an answer to a commonly asked question, or a brief how-to tutorial. Because its value is not time-dependent, you can refer back to it in future blog posts, and other bloggers will link to it and refer people to it over and over again. Yaro highlights his pillar articles in a "Popular Articles" section in his blog header.

A pillar article will bring in a flood of traffic when first released, often because of people linking to or trackbacking your article and generating a little bit of "buzz" around the blogosphere, and the traffic keeps coming long after the article is archived deep within your blog. Pillar articles often rank well in search engines and bring brand-new readers to your blog long after you first published the article.

New visitors to your blog are much more likely to bookmark your site or subscribe to your RSS feed once they see all your fantastic content. "They will start monitoring your blog regularly, transforming from casual random surfer into loyal reader, because they can see the quality of your previous work," says Yaro.

Many techniques are available for driving more traffic to a blog, but without having pillars in place, most of these techniques will be effective only temporarily. If you do nothing else for your blog but write quality content, you will get traffic.

Yaro, like most other blog experts, suggests some planning before starting to blog and produce content. "You do not have to have a concrete reason, but at least have a direction and purpose for blogging," recommends Yaro. "Are you doing it for money? For fun? For fame? To help land a job or sell a product or launch a book?"

A crucial part of planning is having a target audience. You need a target audience to produce quality content for. Targeted traffic is the real key to successful blogging. Ten readers who want what you offer are better than 100 remotely interested readers. "Those 100 won't stick around for very long, nor will they likely buy/subscribe/join or do whatever it is your blog asks them to do," says Yaro, "but the ten targeted readers will very likely do what you want them to do." They'll also become fans and tell other people about you, sending more traffic in your direction.

"I think almost any blogger writing about any topic who devotes himself or herself to building a great blog will enjoy continued traffic growth," insists Yaro, for the amount of people coming online continues to grow. "If you offer value to a marketplace, your traffic will continue to grow as long as that marketplace exists and your value remains."

62. E-MAIL BLOG INTERFACES

Giving readers options

■ ■ ■

I had a great conversation with Phil Hollows, founder of FeedBlitz, *www.feedblitz.com,* a service that monitors blogs, RSS feeds, and Web URLs and provides an e-mail interface for content delivery. All e-mail interfaces for blogs work in basically the same way: They allow you to automatically generate a small piece of code that gets added to your blog, which allows users to sign up and have new blog posts automatically e-mailed to them. These interfaces differ greatly in options, support, and reliability, however, and FeedBlitz has been one of the most successful.

Some veteran bloggers will probably say, "E-mail interfaces for blogs—that's silly. You should be using RSS." Many people who aren't technically savvy may understand e-mail, however, but may be intimidated or turned off by RSS or Atom or feed readers. E-mail is comfortable and ubiquitous—people of all ages and backgrounds use and depend on it. According to Phil, an e-mail interface will typically boost readership 10 percent, and in some blogs, it's been much more—in some cases well over 100% percent.

An e-mail interface will also allow you to use blogging software to manage content, without using the term *"blog."* Just as less tech-savvy users may cringe at a mention of RSS, they may not care or want to hear about blogs, but they do care about content.

An e-mail interface, together with blog software, provides a very easy way to publish and deliver newsletter content online. And because Feed-Blitz adheres to good e-mail marketing principles, including double opt-in, which requires users to subscribe and then confirm their subscription, it's essentially spam-free.

Another potential use of e-mail interfaces is replacing group e-mail lists with a blog and e-mail feed. Migrating to blogging software with an e-mail interface has advantages, including a permanent record of every message as a blog post.

My conversation with Phil is making me rethink some of my current practices. For example, I have an e-zine, an electronic magazine or newsletter, called BizBlog+, but why? Well, marketing wizards agree you need to "capture" e-mail addresses. Why "capture" anything? I just want people to read what I write, including my marketing messages. Why shouldn't BizBlog+ simply be a blog with an e-mail interface?

How popular is the idea of an e-mail interface for blogs? Well, after just six months of existence, FeedBlitz served well over 20,000 blogs and 300,000 readers! It's incredibly popular. This is, no doubt, in part because FeedBlitz's basic service is free, but it does clearly demonstrate the popularity of this idea.

63. FEEDS—
EASY, CONVENIENT, AND
FAST ACCESS TO NEW CONTENT

Blogs and syndication

■ ■ ■

"RSS use is skyrocketing," says Bill Flitter, founder and vice president of marketing of Pheedo Inc., an RSS and Web log marketing solutions company.

Bill, like most people, uses RSS as a generic term to encompass all types of feeds, including different versions of RSS and the similar Atom specification. A feed is simply a channel of information; more concretely, it's a file that contains all the new or recent content from a blog or other Web site.

People can use a feed reader such as MyYahoo!, Bloglines, or FeedDemon, or an RSS-aware browser such as Firefox or Internet Explorer 7.0 to access the information in feeds. This allows readers to consume more information more effectively, for they don't need to visit their favorite blogs and other RSS-enabled sites to see if there is anything new.

The Bloglines feed reader is shown in Figure 5.1 as an example. It's currently displaying new posts from Dan Janal's PR LEADS Blog.

FIGURE 5.1 Bloglines Feed Reader

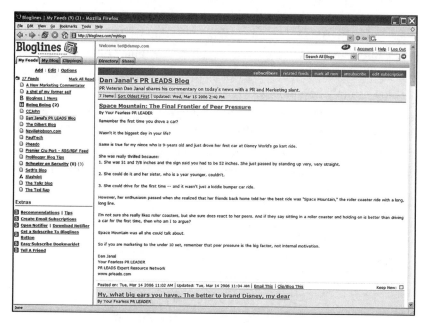

"You don't need a blog to have a feed," says Bill. This is a popular misconception, but many sites that are not blogs have feeds, including Web sites for retailers and news agencies like USA Today and Reuters.

We're seeing an evolution, Bill believes. "Publishers never wanted content online—they all do now," Bill says. We've certainly seen that with media: Most newspapers have Web sites and their material is available online, usually for free. Most media outlets have learned to capitalize on their online presence and content, for example, through advertising.

"Now publishers don't want RSS—they want readers to visit their Web site," according to Bill, "but this will also change." Some publishers use "summary feeds"—only part of each piece of information, such as a newspaper headline or partial blog post, is included in the feed. Readers need to click through to the Web site to see the whole article. This may be backfiring, for Bill's unscientific analysis of his company's data indicates that click-through rates, and resulting visits to the publisher's Web site, are approximately twice as high for full-text feeds!

RSS advertising, just like RSS, is in its infancy. RSS ads can be attached to content, such as a blog post, or can be stand-alone items in a feed. Today, the typical RSS user is a higher-income, technically-savvy person, although that will doubtlessly change as RSS becomes more widely adopted. In the future, a successful advertising campaign won't live only in the feeds, as RSS advertisements do today, but will be integrated with the entire user experience.

RSS itself will be changing and evolving. Today, signing up for an RSS feed requires no registration or user information. Bill sees that changing, and believes that in the future, subscriptions will require some personal information, as needed when subscribing to an e-mail newsletter. He also believes that RSS will also have many additional uses: for example, RSS will replace some e-mail exchanges. No, e-mail is not going away, but RSS will replace some communications that take place over e-mail, such as e-mail groups.

RSS is not going away—it's just too valuable and convenient. Its use is exploding, at least in part because of its integration with browsers and Microsoft's Vista operating system. Its name may change to something more user-friendly, its use will become more widespread, and Bill believes it will be one of the main conduits for information access on the Internet.

64. TRACKING BLOG STATISTICS

The numbers are important

■ ■ ■

Easton Ellsworth is the blog network editor for the Know More Media blog network, which has approximately 45 authors, 55 blogs, and more than 100 posts a day, and is growing rapidly. His responsibilities include writing BusinessBlogWire, *www.businessblogwire.com,* acting as a resource for all the other bloggers, getting new authors started, and tracking blog statistics across the entire network.

Know More Media tracks statistics closely but doesn't have any specific numerical goals other than a general upward growth of traffic. Easton currently uses three free tools to track statistics, both across the blog network as a whole and for individual blogs themselves. The three tools are SiteMeter, Google Analytics, and Feedburner.

Easton uses the free version of SiteMeter—SiteMeter also has an enhanced version, SiteMeter Plus, that offers additional features for $59 a year. SiteMeter tracks both statistics per blog and statistics for the whole network. Easton finds referrals data (where readers are coming from) and entry pages information (what page visitors use to enter a blog) are two of the most interesting, and often surprising, reports. SiteMeter also tracks how many visits and page views there are per day, week, and month. Easton also likes the month-to-month big picture graphical views, which show trends very well.

Google Analytics, which is also free, is used to analyze information at a more granular level. In particular, Google Analytics is used to track what keywords users are searching on to find specific posts in the Know More Media network. Easton says he is "sometimes shocked" at the terms and how highly various pages rank for them.

FeedBurner is used to track readers accessing blogs via RSS or Atom, such as those users using feed readers like MyYahoo!, Bloglines, Pluck, or Firefox Live Bookmarks. Easton uses the free version of FeedBurner. Feed-Burner also has a paid version with more features. "Personally, I love it," says Easton. "It's the Swiss army knife of feed statistics." It tracks such information as how many readers are viewing via feeds, which posts they are clicking through to, what types of feed readers they are using, and much more. FeedBurner also transparently handles any compatibility issues between different types and versions of feeds, and there are several.

The processes of implementing SiteMeter, Google Analytics, and FeedBurner are similar. They all require you to sign up for an account, and they all offer free accounts. You then need to add a small snippet of HTML code to your blog(s). Simple instructions are included, and any blog/Webmaster can do it easily. And all three can track Web site statistics as well as blog statistics.

Easton is happy with the tools he is using and the wealth of free data they reveal about blog traffic and readers, but he adds that he's "always looking for better tools."

65. TRACKING AND OPTIMIZING FEEDS WITH FEEDBURNER

What's happening in your feeds?

■ ■ ■

FeedBurner describes itself as the "world's largest feed management provider." It provides both free and more advanced paid services to bloggers, podcasters, and commercial publishers.

Mike Sansone, a blogging consultant and copywriter who describes himself as a "conversation director," has been using FeedBurner since he started blogging. "The great thing about FeedBurner is that you can track what goes on in your feed," says Mike. With more and more people accessing blogs, podcasts, and more via feeds, this is becoming more and more important. "Standard statistics packages don't track this information."

FeedBurner tells you the number of subscribers you have, which posts have been clicked on and how many times, what feed readers subscribers are using to read your feed, and much more. Mike suggests looking at your feed with the most popular feed readers to see what your feed looks like in them, just like you might use the most popular Web browsers to see how your Web site appears in them.

Feeds are implemented via different versions of RSS, Atom, and more, but who really wants to understand or even think about this? Well, your blog or podcast almost certainly has some kind of feed already, and with FeedBurner you can entirely ignore feed types and versions by publishing a "SmartFeed™" This automatically takes care of any translation and compatibility issues.

Many blogs, podcasts, and Web sites will end up with multiple feeds, including a FeedBurner SmartFeed. Because of the "auto-discovery" of feeds, which automatically finds a feed from a given URL, it's important to make sure all your feed offerings are through FeedBurner. This allows FeedBurner to track all your feed statistics. This involves a simple change to your blog's HTML code, and simple steps are included on the Feed-Burner Web site.

What about helping to promote your feed? "FeedFlare allows you to put links within your feed," says Mike. "'E-mail This' and 'Add to Del.icio.us' are among the most popular. You can also write your own Feed-Flare to point your audience to other offerings, such as a book, a survey, or your contact information." Once again, this involves a simple change to your blog's HTML code.

FeedBurner can do other things, such as allowing you to easily publish your feed on a static Web page, place advertisements in your feed, and much more.

Feeds are becoming more important as they become more popular. Tracking feed statistics and optimizing feeds is important. Mike summarizes with "FeedBurner is the tool I recommend to business leaders and consumers alike due to its ease of use. FeedBurner also stays ahead of other feed publishers by consistently launching new services."

PART 6

PODCAST SPECIFIC TOPICS

■ ■ ■

Podcasts are exploding in number and popularity. The low barrier to entry, the addictive nature, and the incredible amount of both niche and mainstream content are hard to beat—yet not everyone is upbeat. Some people see podcasting itself as a niche technology, never to approach "traditional" text-based blogging in popularity. They see many of podcasting's most enthusiastic supporters as those who missed the first wave of blogging and are looking for "the next big thing."

Certainly podcasting is growing and podcasts are evolving. New podcasts are started every week. People even argue about what exactly a podcast is—is it always audio or can it be video? Not all users like audio. Some prefer watching video. Some prefer reading and are more comfortable with blogs. People have different learning styles and preferences.

We're going to hear some thoughts and advice from podcast fans and pioneers, and then look at some examples of podcasts themselves. You'll also find podcasting information throughout this book. This chapter deals with podcast specifics that don't apply to text-based blogs.

66.

WHAT MAKES A GREAT PODCAST?

Advice for podcasters

■ ■ ■

So what makes a great podcast? Who better to ask than Paul Gillin, an independent content marketing consultant and former IT journalist who is an enormous fan of podcasts?

"A great podcast is short and passionate," says Paul. The ideal length is between 5 and 20 minutes, and at 30 minutes a podcaster is risking overstaying his or her welcome. People prefer shorter podcasts. Longer podcasts can work well if the podcaster has a very strong personality, such as Adam Curry and his popular Daily Source Code podcast, *www.dailysourcecode.com,* or if the podcast is a recording of a live event, for example, a speech at a conference.

"Podcasters need to be passionate about their topic," adds Paul. There must be an intersection between the strengths of the podcaster and the podcast's format so that passion shows through. For example, some people may be more effective and comfortable podcasting in a question-and-answer format or with a cohost, while others may be more effective taking a more casual approach.

Five formats for podcasts work well, according to Paul:

1. One person talking

2. Question-and-answer format with a subject matter expert

3. Cohosted podcasts, with personalities that have complementary strengths and play off each other well

4. A news format, which works especially well in underserved, and often very specialized, markets

5. Speeches of recorded events, such as conferences and other meetings

Enormous numbers of new podcasts are appearing, and Paul has some very sensible advice to anyone looking at starting a podcast:

- Pick something you are passionate about.

- Plan six to eight podcasts with the basics of what you know.

- Have some ideas of how to continue when you run out of obvious things to talk about.

Businesses that want to start a podcast must conduct some research first, just as businesses that want to start a blog must do some research. They need to listen to a variety of podcasts to explore different formats and techniques. They also need to pick a great topic they are passionate about. And quite important for a business podcast, it needs a purpose, not just "Let's podcast because everyone else is doing it."

A business topic need not mirror a company's core business, but the topic should be relevant for the business's audience. An example is the popular American Family podcasts, *www.whirlpool.com/custserv/promo.jsp?sectionId=563,* from Whirlpool. They don't talk about appliances; it's hard to imagine an interesting series of podcasts on washing machines! These podcasts concentrate on family issues, and presumably many families buy appliances, at least as compared to single people in their 20s! Recent topics include homeschooling, baby food, and children's playdates.

An enormous number of really good podcasts exists—so many that you could probably listen 24 hours a day. If you want your podcast to succeed and become really popular, it needs to be more than really good; it needs to be great!

67. EVERYONE SHOULD PODCAST

Or at least have an audio presence on the Internet

■ ■ ■

"All solopreneurs should podcast," says Michael Pollack, an Internet business consultant who thinks all businesses should be podcasting. Although he may be exaggerating slightly, Michael makes a number of great points and observations.

"Portability is part of today's lifestyle," notes Michael. People have limited time to read a brochure, book, or surf the Web, but there is a lot of available time while moving—both while driving and during other activities when one cannot read. Satellite radio capitalizes on this trend, and so do other forms of audio such as podcasts, which allow users with scarce reading time to listen while they are driving, walking the dog, or exercising.

Audio has another big benefit besides portability—familiarity. People may come to feel they know you from reading your blog, but they more quickly become familiar with you when they hear your voice. "A lot is communicated via voice," says Michael.

"We're getting out of the early adopter phase, and podcasts are rapidly becoming more mainstream," according to Michael. "Podcasts, or at least some audio presence, will quickly become almost necessary for conducting business, just as business cards have long been essentially required and just about every company has a Web site today." Podcasting is developing into less of an opportunity and more of a requirement. Not having an audio presence is quickly becoming a competitive disadvantage.

The number of devices that can play MP3s, the common podcast file format, is rapidly growing. Specialized audio devices are relatively cheap and the prices are dropping rapidly, and MP3 audio capability is increasingly being integrated into other devices. Many new cars have built-in MP3 players, just as all cars have some kind of radio. "Even two years ago, high-end RVs had MP3 players built in," says Michael. Before long, the now ubiquitous cell phone will have integrated MP3 functionality. "Within five years, everyone will have an audio device, just like everyone has a TV and radio today," notes Michael. Of course, most computers can also play MP3 files, although they are not usually mobile or convenient.

It's easy and inexpensive to start podcasting. Michael records on his PC, using a couple of different programs. Many cheap and free programs are available. An easy way to start podcasting is to interview experts in your field and related fields. Michael usually conducts podcast interviews over Skype, and uses the free version of the HotRecorder product to record them.

Before long, having an audio presence on the Internet will be almost a requirement for doing business. Fortunately, podcasting is an easy and inexpensive way to get audio on the Internet.

68. SOME PODCASTING ADVICE

At a minimum: passion, a desire to share, and time

■ ■ ■

"Don't do it to make money," says Martin McKeay, a security expert who is involved with two podcasts, his Network Security podcast, *www.mckeay.net,* and The Podcast Roundtable, *www.podcastround table.com.* Maybe the top 1 percent of podcasts are profitable, and planning on making money is not a reasonable goal. There are plenty of other business, personal, and social reasons to podcast, according to Martin.

Podcasting develops relationships and creates opportunities you'd never have otherwise. There are chances to interview people and attend events you never would have otherwise. Martin has met plenty of famous and well-known people because of his podcasting. The networking opportunities are immense. As someone once said, "It's not what you know, it's who you know," and podcasters tend to know a lot of people and are well known. Also, just "the exchange of ideas is worth the time put into it," adds Martin.

Martin suggests you had better be passionate about your podcasting topic, and it should be something you want to share. Don't just do it because it's a fad! If you're not passionate or don't want to share, you probably won't keep doing it or succeed. "Many people don't realize the time involved," according to Martin. He often starts working on his Network Security Podcast around 7 PM and finishes at midnight. His 30-minute podcast takes one to two hours of preparation time, 30 to 45 minutes of recording, one to two more hours of postproduction work, and then an additional hour for uploading, producing show notes, and other miscellaneous tasks. That's up to 5 or more hours to produce a 30-minute podcast!

Martin prefers to podcast with others. "I'm boring by myself," says Martin, although his listeners might disagree. Martin likes having guests on his Network Security podcast, someone to bounce ideas off, and finds it really allows for an expansion of ideas. Many podcasters agree with Martin, and podcasts often have multiple hosts as well as guests.

The Podcast Roundtable has five hosts, all bloggers, who have enough different viewpoints on the Internet and Web to make it worthwhile to get together each month and talk. At least 700 people agree and download the monthly podcast. Multiple hosts keep it lively and interesting.

With multiple hosts, however, Martin says there will certainly be additional challenges. Everyone needs to have similar goals. They don't need to be identical, but they must align somewhat. With multiple hosts, it is especially important to plan up front in what direction the podcast will be going. Although the plan may certainly evolve, there must be some basic agreement among the members. It's also possible that interpersonal issues may be involved and things just may not work out in the long term.

Podcasting is time-intensive, and you must be passionate about your topic and want to share. It can also be incredibly rewarding with networking opportunities, the chance to exchange ideas, and more. Just don't start podcasting to join the fad and don't plan on generating direct revenue. Do some basic planning, and do it for the long term. Martin suggests the only way to start is just to do it—too many people plan and never start, or start and never feel their podcasts are good enough to put on the Internet, and that benefits no one.

69. TALKR—CONVERTING BLOGS TO PODCASTS

Listening to text-based blogs while driving

■ ■ ■

Imagine driving to the office as you read your favorite blogs. Sound like insanity, a dream, or fantasy? Many users regularly listen to podcasts in the car, but can't keep up with blogs while driving, or at least they couldn't before Talkr, *www.talkr.com.*

Talkr founder Chris Brooks had the same problems. He used to commute to work, wasting three hours each day in the process. He tried to use the time effectively, listening to podcasts and audio books, but he would fall behind on his reading, especially blogs. A three-hour commute is not that uncommon in the United States, and certainly scores of people spend at least an hour a day driving to and from work. Just an hour a day means that 250 hours are spent commuting in a typical work year.

Chris came up with a way to easily convert blogs to podcasts and listen to them while commuting. "Talkr podcasts the blogs you love," says Chris. "It's a podcasting server." You can hear your favorite blogs at times when reading is inappropriate or impossible, like while you are driving, exercising, or mowing the lawn. Many busy people have very limited additional reading time most weeks, but have free listening time when they are busy doing other things—and they can now use that extra "ear time" to catch up on their favorite blogs.

Many users may be a bit apprehensive, recalling that early attempts at converting text to audio were, well, clumsy, with robotic and not entirely understandable voices requiring extreme concentration. In contrast, Talkr's voice is a pleasant and inviting female voice. It is slightly robotic, but not unpleasantly so, and very listenable.

Talkr offers both free and paid services. The free service allows you to listen to Talkr's free audio feeds, about 16 popular blogs, as well as any three additional blogs you chose. Actually, Talkr will let you listen to more than just blogs—it can convert any Web site with an RSS feed into audio.

You can also add "Listen to this post" buttons to your blog by joining the free Talkr Partners program. "Talkr Partners provides bloggers with a podcast of their text-only blog," says Chris. "Once configured, the day-to-day process of producing the podcast is fully automated. Talkr provides hosting and bandwidth for the podcast." Talkr also offers paid services with additional features.

Our lives today provide us with little extra time to read! But many people do occasionally have extra "ear time" when driving, biking, in the gym, fishing, or mowing the lawn. Now we can use Talkr to listen to our favorite blogs.

70. MONETIZING PODCASTS

Business models for podcasts

■ ■ ■

"Podcasting is growing at an unprecedented rate," "says Michael Geoghegan, author of the book *Podcast Solutions*. Making money from podcasting is an area of extreme interest, but "podcasters are struggling with monetization," adds Michael. He sees a number of different models for monetizing podcasts, i.e., making money from them, and has succeeded at more than one!

One of the simplest models is when an existing business adds podcasting to their marketing and communications mix. The podcast helps support the business by adding value to the customers, much as business blogging does. Companies podcasting today include Whirlpool, Disney, Cisco, RSA Security, and many more.

Another model is consulting and production services. Big companies who want to podcast rarely have the in-house expertise, but they want to do it right. For example, Michael has produced podcasts for Disney Resorts. The need for consulting and production services for podcasting is growing.

Many podcasters want to monetize their existing or soon-to-be-started podcasts, often on topics they are passionate about, which are not connected to any business. Michael thinks many podcasters have unrealistic expectations, although he does see a lot of opportunity, especially in niche markets. "There are some expectations when you monetize—it's more like a job," says Michael. "It's like the difference between hiring a high school kid to mow your lawn or a lawn-care service." Whether you accept advertisements, sponsors, or product placements, or even charge for your podcast, suddenly you need to give your audience what they want, which may not necessarily be what you always want to do. You may have to commit to a schedule. Details will need to be carefully described in a contract. What if you have a $50-a-week advertiser, and you suddenly get Bill Gates on your podcast? You may suddenly have 250,000 downloads. How long are you required to keep that advertiser or sponsor in your podcast? A week, a month, forever? A good contract will address these issues.

Podcasters must also consider at what price point it makes sense to monetize. Is it worth making the jump for $50 or $100 a week? For the GrapeRadio podcast, *www.graperadio.com,* in which Michael is involved, it was $1,000. Monetizing is hard work and requires contracts, media kits, selling or outsourcing ads and sponsorships, and more.

What are a podcaster's goals when it comes to monetization? It's certainly possible to have podcasting pay for itself and maybe make an extra $5,000 or $10,000 a year, but much harder to quit your day job or get rich. Podcasters need to realize that few will ever quit their day jobs and support themselves solely through podcasting.

There are also nonfinancial rewards from podcasting that may help to make your efforts worthwhile. The GrapeRadio crew gets to travel to wine events worldwide and meet famous wine personalities. Often, they even fly to Southern California specifically to meet with GrapeRadio and be on the show. Michael's Reel Reviews podcast, *www.reelreviewsradio.com,* which reviews movies, results in free DVDs, often before they are released. Podcasters may be treated as members of the media and get access to events they wouldn't otherwise.

A lot of opportunities are appearing in podcasting as it explodes in popularity. Existing companies are leveraging podcasts, and there is work for the podcast-savvy as consultants and in podcast production. The podcast as a media outlet with advertisements, sponsorships, and more can be a viable business model, but podcasters need to set their expectations and realize that making money is usually hard work; previous business experience is helpful.

71. WHAT DO PODCAST LISTENERS WANT?

Feedback is elusive

■ ■ ■

"A lot of people are getting involved in podcasting and they are taking a 'Record it and they will come' attitude," says Dan Sweet, who is in the IT services and staffing industry. "But attracting an audience is difficult." Dan's podcast is the Free Resume And Career Toolbox podcast, FRACAT, *www.fracat.com/blog,* where he covers job-seeking and career topics. He also is a host of the Podcast Roundtable, *www.podcastroundtable.com,* a podcast where five people comment on the Internet and the Web.

Dan receives a lot of positive feedback on his podcasting, which is great. Unfortunately, the vast majority of comments are along the lines of "Excellent show" or "I love the podcast." Other podcasters have similar experiences. These aren't comments that help fine-tune the content or direction of the podcasts. The number of people listening is growing for both podcasts, but there is little information about what people are looking for. That type of feedback has been essentially impossible to get.

"It's like trying to mine for gold in the dark," says Dan. Perhaps people aren't sure what they want from podcasting. Maybe you can survey your current listeners—but how about everyone else out there? If you pick a specialization that has lots of interest, especially if you are the first or among the first in that niche, then you'll have plenty of listeners, but luck also plays a large role.

Doing something you love is great, but "you are not your own market," stresses Dan. Don't assume that because you like something, other people will, too. You need to produce content that your listeners and target market like, and figuring out what that is can be difficult.

Another challenge is attracting people in addition to those who are already podcast-savvy. Most people don't know, and may not care, what a podcast is. Some factors to consider are where your target audience hangs out, what they read, etc. If they are young, for example, MySpace might work. One hint may be to avoid using the term *"podcast."* Several success-ful podcasts have the term *"radio"* in their name, like GrapeRadio. People are familiar and comfortable with the term *radio.*

The barriers to entry in podcasting are low and almost anyone can pro-duce a podcast. That is part of its attraction. But the vast amounts of mate-rial that are created can make it difficult to attract listeners. Creativity can be highly rewarded. No one knows exactly what works or will work in the future. In the short term, Dan is podcasting and not worrying too much about his numbers of listeners. They are increasing, so he must be provid-ing value, but getting feedback on what they want remains somewhat elu-sive.

72.   PODSAFE MUSIC

The Podsafe Music Network

■ ■ ■

Music licensing bodies have not embraced podcasting, to say the least. Many copyright and licensing policies were created in reaction to concerns about illegal file sharing, and they haven't been changed since. "When the record labels, the RIAA, licensing bodies, and others hear MP3, they freak out," says C. C. Chapman, podsafe music advocate and prolific podcaster. They don't understand podcasting. "It can be dangerous for podcasters to play music," warns C. C.

In late 2004, C. C. started a music podcast. It was fun, but not worth getting sued over, so he convinced unsigned bands to agree to have their music played on his podcast. It was hard: He had to find the bands. He had to exchange countless e-mails. He had to continually explain what podcasting was.

In early 2005, PodShow, *www.podshow.com,* a podcast network, tapped C. C. to create a repository of podsafe music that any podcast could use without fear of legal action. What exactly is podsafe music? C. C. defines it as "music that all the rights holders have said can be used license-free on podcasts." Podsafe music is important for more than music podcasts, because many nonmusic podcasts use music during their introductions or closings.

Podcasts and podsafe music are very empowering for artists. They can release all or some of their music as podsafe, and they get exposure, they get heard, and they can sell their music worldwide. C. C. related a story in which a beginning podsafe artist in Tennessee was amazed that someone from Australia was ordering his CD; it's a great source of exposure with no cost to the artist.

Royalties through the traditional channels are slim—the artists get a small percentage of the proceeds from the sales of CDs and other media. In contrast, when artists sell music directly to their fans, they keep all the profit. Most artists need to do their own promotion whether they are selling music directly to fans or not. Record companies rarely do promotion, particularly for emerging artists: They just get the CDs into stores.

The Podsafe Music Network, *music.podshow.com,* went live in July of 2005. It currently has more than 4,000 artists and 20,000 songs. Many successful bands are interested and have made some of their music available. The smaller independent record labels are on board, and many midsize ones are too. As for the bigger record companies, "I'd rather work with them," says C. C., but they tend to be litigious instead of friendly. Artists who have contracts with them could be getting exposure and potentially increasing sales by releasing some of their music as podsafe.

The labels need artists more than artists need labels today. A record contract has never been an assurance of success, and it is becoming less and less important. In the end, podcasting and podsafe music is part of the marketing for many bands. It helps get the word and the music out.

73. PROMOTING MUSIC THROUGH PODCASTING

Brother Love

■ ■ ■

"It's been pretty fantastic," says Brother Love, a pop-rock singer and songwriter. "It's the wave of the future, or maybe the future is now." He's talking about his experiences promoting his music through podcasting, both on his own podcast, Brother Love Notes, *brotherlovenotes.blogspot.com,* and via other podcasts and the Podsafe Music Network. He believes this is the best way for unsigned, up-and-coming artists to promote themselves.

In mid-2005, a friend suggested, "You gotta check out podcasting." Brother Love checked it out and contacted a podcaster with a request to play his music. On successive days, his music was played on PodcastNYC, *www.podcastnyc.net,* Getting a Leg Up, *legup.libsyn.com,* Accident Hash, *accidenthash.podshow.com,* and Daily Source Code, *www.dailysourcecode. com.* You may recognize some of these as extremely popular podcasts.

"I started making money," says Brother Love. "I realized the power of it." His CD, available on *www.CDbaby.com,* which connects with iTunes and many other distribution points, started selling. He began earning a few hundred dollars every week or two.

He also put a couple of songs on the Podsafe Music Network. He realized he was giving away his intellectual property in exchange for worldwide distribution. "It's all about getting your music out there," says Brother Love. Podcasters gave links to Brother Love's Web site, *www.brotherloverocks.com,* in their show notes in exchange. He was becoming well known and receiving lots of fan e-mail.

In November of 2005, he was flying to the Podcast and Portable Media Expo and was shocked when people recognized him on the plane. "That was when I really got it," says Brother Love. "Now I have friends. It's like a small army." Whenever he is playing a gig, podcasters play recordings of him asking fans to come to the show, and it works well.

Brother Love's music is all over the place. Podcasting has helped put it on the map. It has been in a motion picture and may be appearing in TV commercials and shows soon, and, of course, there's his CD, his live shows, his contributions to the Podsafe Music Network, and plenty of podcasts that play his music.

Would Brother Love be interested in a record company contract if it were offered? "It would have to be a pretty damn good contract," he states. "I'm my own record label at this point."

74. WAXXI, AN INTERACTIVE PODCAST MODEL

Building community with scheduled podcasts and social media

■ ■ ■

Many argue that podcasts are one-way and there really is little conversation. Podcasts are recorded and posted, and afterward, people can listen. Others disagree, arguing that podcasters often read comments and play audio comments from previous shows. But these comments are after the show; they are not interactive. A podcast is not as interactive as, for example, talk radio. There is certainly far less of a conversation—nothing in real time.

"We let people be part of the conversation," says Tracy A. Sheridan, CEO of Waxxi, *www.waxxi.us.* "They can ask questions as well as make comments." Waxxi runs scheduled interactive podcasts, and listeners can call in, toll-free in the United States, in real time. "The audience also gets to interact with each other," adds Tracy. Participants can use an embedded chat client to interact without needing to call. Guests see the chat and interact as well. "They have a feeling of closeness and connection with the audience," she adds, "which is much stronger than with a 'traditional podcast.'" Podcasts are also archived and available later.

Waxxi is also launching a business-focused global social network that will allow participants to converse outside of scheduled podcasts. They'll also be able to create profiles with information about themselves and their interests. Groups are being formed around the interactive podcast topics, including business blogging, Web 2.0, and more. Groups can also be formed from the suggestions of participants.

Waxxi's inaugural podcast featured authors and well-known bloggers Robert Scoble and Shel Israel on the theme of business blogging. Participants registered for the event on Waxxi's Web site and were given a unique user code and telephone number to dial in. The conversation was moderated to avoid "podcast chaos"—people had to raise their hands by touching two buttons on their telephone to ask a question. Waxxi allows 800 people, but will soon have the capability to allow 5,000, in its podcasts. There was a lively back channel conversation via chat.

There will be no shortage of opportunities for Waxxi going forward, for both informative and community-building events, as well as for organizations to use internally and with their customers and partners. Social media is evolving, and Waxxi is part of that ongoing evolution.

75. THE NEW RULES OF PODCASTING

Podcasting—there really are no rules

■ ■ ■

"There really are no rules—I can do anything I want with this," thought Rob Safuto when he first discovered podcasting. "How liberating this is!" Rob is the podcast producer and consultant responsible for Podcast NYC, *www.podcastnyc.net,* and others.

Unfortunately, some de facto rules started to creep in. The longer you had been podcasting, and the more podcasts you'd produced, the "cooler" you were. At the Podcast Expo last year, someone belittled a friend of his who had produced only six podcasts so far. "But they're really good podcasts," said Rob. Apparently, quantity is more important than quality to many podcasters. It was also assumed that once you started podcasting you had to do it for life, or you failed. Rob can think of several short-term podcasting models that can work, such as a series of podcasts to promote an event.

Rob has started writing "The New Rules of Podcasting" at the Podcast NYC blog, *www.podcastnyc.net/blog.* These are partly a reaction to the rules many podcasters seem to accept and also an effort to help people who are new to podcasting. Rob is not negative: He sees lots of great things happening in podcasting, but he also sees confusion, bad practices, and charlatans attempting to profit from other's efforts in podcasting. I spoke to Rob about his favorite new rules.

1. Signing away the exclusive rights to your podcast is a stupid thing to do. Some podcasters are signing away exclusive rights for a contract that promises nothing more than free hosting, and hosting is pretty cheap. "Some contracts are laughable," says Rob, "and even require you sign away your name, likeness, and any ideas attributed to your podcast." If they were paying real money, they might be worth considering.

Rob suggests you podcast for at least a year and hone your craft. Try to develop a minibrand. If you're proud of your podcast, try to line up nonexclusive agreements. You can also try to find sponsors directly. Your podcast may be worthless commercially, or you may become an enormous star. Why sign away all your rights for next to nothing?

2. Networks are a losing business model. Podcast networks are hot, but do they make sense? A podcast network can serve several purposes, including offering podcasters a business and technical infrastructure, for example helping podcasts make money and hosting the podcast files themselves, and offering listeners a single source of many high-quality podcasts. "In traditional media, networks can work because growth of new outlets is constrained," says Rob, "but not so in podcasting." It's not easy to start a new TV station, but there are new podcasts created every day—their growth is unrestrained. There is a flood of new content and trying to organize existing podcasts into a network doesn't make much sense.

Advertising is a primary reason that networks are advocated. Sponsors can advertise across an entire network instead of writing lots of little checks to separate podcasts, but Rob doesn't buy that argument. He believes advertisers will "start producing their own podcasts instead of taking their chances on a ragtag bunch of indie media producers who might just screw up their message," and any money that flows into networks will be extremely diluted before it gets to individual podcasts.

Rob does believe that aggregating like content into a network to build community and make it easy to find makes sense, and gives the Culinary Podcast Network, *www.culinarypodcastnetwork.com,* as a great example. But a network of a little of this and a little of that—what benefit does that provide for podcasters or for their audience?

3. Demographics don't matter. People worry too much about audience demographics, but the model is very different than traditional media. With all the choices in podcasting, audiences tend to be very interested in the topic they're listening to. Would you rather have a few thousand intermittent, somewhat interested listeners, or a few hundred who are dedicated and are passionate about the topic?

4. Revolutionary change will come out of nowhere. Rob believes that big things and big changes are in store for podcasting. "Someone will come out of nowhere with something no one has ever thought of and take the world by storm," he exclaims. "It'll really reach into the public consciousness. There is no formula and no amount of money will help." It'll just be someone with an amazing new idea.

76.   MANIC MOMMIES

Creating community for working moms
through a podcast, blog, and private group

■ ■ ■

"Working moms do crave to connect with others, and it's global," says Kristin Brandt. "There is a real hunger for working moms to connect with each other. Stay-at-home moms have far more opportunities to connect with each other at kids' events and play dates." Manic Mommies, *www.manicmommies.com,* helps working moms connect.

In 2005, Erin Kane, another working mom, told Kristin they should start a podcast together and talk about being working moms. Kristen says she "got into it to find out what it was all about." They also started a Manic Mommies blog. Kristen had previously started a blog, but it had failed because she had no focus and had trouble deciding what to write about. In comparison, focusing on working-mom issues made it easy.

Initially, they podcasted monthly, but eventually went weekly. Both Kristin and Erin have full-time jobs in the communications field, and podcasting is a significant time commitment: "It's a hobby, so it's hard to give it the attention it deserves." The average 45-minute show takes 5 hours to create. It's a lot of work, and they are highly dedicated. It's only possible because they both have very tolerant and supportive husbands.

The response has been terrific. "Our audience amazes me," adds Kristin. "We never ever would have anticipated this type of response." They often get long, personal e-mails from listeners asking for advice. They ran a recent contest in which listeners needed to send in a secret word from the podcast, and 99 percent of them sent the word (*"medicine"*) and introductory e-mails as well.

Besides the podcast and blog, Kristin and Erin have set up a private group on *www.gather.com* to further help their listeners connect and give them a chance to start conversations. *Gather.com* has been described as MySpace for older, educated people, and members must sign up and be approved. Any member can post anything, including text and pictures.

"Manic Mommies has been incredibly rewarding," says Kristen. Making money was never a goal, although they have recently started looking for sponsors.

So, once a week, when the kids are in bed, Erin and Kristin get together, drink wine or cosmopolitans, and share their trials and tribulations with moms and dads around the world. And they further the community they're creating through their blog and private group on *gather.com.*

77. THE FINANCIAL AID PODCAST

Promoting the Student Loan Network

■ ■ ■

Every day the Financial Aid Podcast, *www.financialaidpodcast.com,* now well beyond show 300, gives advice on financial aid, personal finance, and scholarships, and more than 2,300 people listen. "It's a promotional vehicle for the Student Loan Network," says Christopher Penn, the producer and CTO of the Student Loan Network. "It's been directly attributable for $250,000 in loans so far."

It started as an internal podcast for employees and was spurred by two events: Christopher got an iPod just as podcasting came on his radar and the company had "an employee who needed to hear things more than once," he says charitably. After the first five or six podcasts in 2005, it became clear that the podcasts contained information that would have value to others.

The original format interspersed podsafe music with information, but Christopher sometimes found himself fast-forwarding through the music, so he changed the format to have the music follow the information. Podcasts often contain music, and because his target audience includes high school and college students, it's particularly appropriate.

Christopher promotes the Financial Aid Podcast in a number of ways. He submits audio comments to other podcasts, including the popular podcasts

Adam Curry's Daily Source Code and Accident Hash by C. C. Chapman. Whenever his podcast is mentioned, he gets a flood of additional traffic.

"MySpace guerrilla marketing has made an enormous difference," Christopher adds. MySpace is a social networking site that's enormously popular among students. When someone visits his MySpace site, the podcast starts playing automatically. "The stealth secret weapon in MySpace is finding bands and supporting them," he says. "Support them and they'll support you." It's certainly working: The Financial Aid Podcast has more than 19,000 "friends" in MySpace, although he admits that the MySpace definition of a friend is fairly loose.

The Financial Aid Podcast is also syndicated and available on some colleges' traditional radio stations. Christopher is pursuing syndication to additional college stations to further increase his audience.

What would Christopher do differently if he were starting now? Not much: He says he'd market more aggressively initially and start with better podcasting equipment.

Christopher is having a lot of success with his podcast. He offers value to his target audience, and some become customers. He's going to where his target audience hangs out and listens: MySpace, iTunes, and college radio stations. He's doing a lot of things very right, and the Student Loan Network is certainly benefiting financially from his efforts.

78. RIGHTLOOK RADIO

Podcasting to sell
automobile-reconditioning equipment

■ ■ ■

"It was a no-brainer," says Stephen Powers, president of Rightlook. "No question it would work for Rightlook!" Steven is talking about podcasting to support his business, which provides automobile-reconditioning equipment and training. Most of his sales are in the "Auto Detailing" space.

Many of his customers are looking to start a business. They are entrepreneurs who may spend $25,000 to $35,000 at once. Sales of this size
require building trust. Rightlook already had an extremely informative Web
site. Adding a podcast to help build trust made perfect sense, for its customers want as much information as they can get.

A potential customer talks to a salesperson, but that's just the beginning. The salesperson points them to Rightlook Radio, *www.rightlookra-
dio.com*. Or they might find the podcast from the Web site, catalog, or
maybe from a Rightlook ad in an industry publication. Some of them stay
up half the night listening.

What kind of content can be that compelling? Steven and cohost Mel
Craig talk about opportunities in the industry, interview successful automo-
bile-detailing company owners, explain new add-on services that can be
provided, discuss business issues such as the importance of professional-
ism, and more. In other words, they provide the kind of information their
target market wants—information to help them succeed in the auto-recon-
ditioning business.

Stephen invested about $5,000 on equipment when he started. He got
Mel to cohost, and he likes the two-host format a lot. "It's more lively, more
entertaining," he says. He also loves interviewing people on the podcast. It
provides lots of great information as well as requiring slightly less prepara-
tory work on the part of the hosts.

Rightlook was already marketing and didn't add any new marketing
when they added the Rightlook Radio podcast. They did start mentioning
Rightlook Radio in their ads, however, and in some cases their existing ads
morphed into Rightlook Radio ads. For example, they've run full-page ads
for Rightlook Radio in industry publications.

So how is it working? Several thousand people listen, and it has absolutely led to sales. "We recently had a customer thinking of going with a
competitor. He was pretty far down that path," says Stephen. "He spent
almost all night listening to Rightlook Radio, and in the morning we had a
$25,000 order." Stephen says that interactions like this one are common.

Rightlook Radio is a great example of using a podcast to help bolster
an existing business. There are plenty of podcasts in the fields of high technology and public relations, but fewer in more traditional fields. Stephen is
getting results and enjoying podcasting as well. He also has the first-mover

advantage in his business. "Normal businesses have been very slow to realize the benefits of podcasts," says Stephen.

79. GRAPERADIO

Guys passionate about wine podcasting

■ ■ ■

When Brian Clark, Leigh Older, and Jay Selman started podcasting, their goals were simple—they initially wanted to have fun. Their podcast "grew rapidly and quickly," according to cohost Brian Clark. "Very quickly there was lots of pressure to do a professional job." Today GrapeRadio, *www.graperadio.com,* has more than 15,000 listeners, is still growing rapidly, and has been mentioned in CNN, *The New York Times, USA Today,* BBC Radio, and *BusinessWeek,* among others. Brian attributes this rapid growth and success to "luck and a good product."

Brian describes GrapeRadio as a "show for people who want to learn about wine," which is both accessible to both wine novices and serious wine connoisseurs. The show has a roundtable format and often features guests, including experts and famous winemakers from around the world. Their list of guests is impressive, and they've always had success getting anyone they wanted as a guest.

They started podcasting in a friend's professional studio and eventually built their own at a cost of $35,000 to $40,000. It's hard producing a show every week, so they also added other cohosts who share their passion for wine.

Shows have included "The Wines of Château Pichon-Longueville Baron," an interview with technical director Jean Rene Matignon (this podcast sent me literally running to my local wine store to experience a bottle of this famous wine), "You Have the Wine List—Now What?" (proper wine etiquette for a business dinner), and the self-explanatory "Trust Your Taste" and "Wine Myths." Each show lasts 30 to 45 minutes and is basic enough to appeal to a novice yet interesting enough to captivate serious oenophiles.

All the cohosts have day jobs, and most are self-employed or own businesses. GrapeRadio brings in $3,000 to $4,000 a month from advertising and sponsors, which covers the costs of trips and equipment. There are a lot of other ways that the GrapeRadio podcast could make money, but, although it may be very professional, it's still a hobby.

So why is this podcast so successful? It is certainly well produced and interesting, has fascinating guests and appeals to a wide body of people interested in wine. No doubt there is some luck involved, as Brian says, but equally important, it's simply extremely well done.

80. MOMMYCAST

An incredibly successful podcast

■ ■ ■

Gretchen Vogelzang's husband "wanted to learn about podcasting, since he's in advertising and marketing and wanted to experiment with the medium." Gretchen had no idea what a podcast was, but once she found out, she thought, "This sounds perfect for mommies! They can catch it whenever and wherever possible—the portability is perfect for mommies." And she knew the perfect person to do it with: fellow mommy Paige Heninger, who was pregnant at the time.

That was in March of 2005. A year later, their listenership was estimated by some at 100,000 or more. They are one of the first podcasts to land a major corporate sponsorship, which can bring in tens of thousands of dollars a month. "Way more money than I ever thought," says Gretchen. They've been interviewed by CNN, NBC, the BBC, *Brandweek,* and *The Wall Street Journal,* and even me! "Podcasting took off far faster than anyone thought it would!" adds Gretchen.

"We're just a couple of mommies," insists Gretchen. So why is the podcast so popular? They talk to each other just like mommies talk to each other—because they are mommies. It's like listening to a telephone call between friends. "People have become so busy," says Gretchen, "they don't have time to hang out in the park or talk on the phone. MommyCast gives mommies a sense of community and camaraderie and lets them know there are others like them. Many people out there are disconnected, maybe away from family."

MommyCast doesn't have advertisements, but they accept two or three sponsors a year who fit in with the show well. For example, Dixie, with their "Make it a Dixie Day," encouraging parents to occasionally use disposable plates, cups, etc., for a day and spend the time saved with their children, fits perfectly with MommyCast. Dixie is their prime sponsor. The sponsorship for Dixie is also ideal because they are perceived as somewhat of an old-fashioned company—"Hey, I remember Dixie cups from when I was a kid." The tight relationship with a popular podcast casts them as cool and modern and fun.

Many people and advertising agencies they talk to don't yet understand the podcast model. They sometimes try to apply metrics that make no sense. Podcasting is very directed—and podcasts hit very specific demographics. It's also not like broadcasting in the sense that people maybe just have a broadcast on in the background. People listen more intently to podcasts.

Gretchen and Paige are pretty much committed to producing two MommyCasts a week now, but "It's still as much fun now that it's professional" comes through loud and clear. Future plans involve extending their brand. For example, they are both interested in music and have started a MommyCast music show that features podsafe music, music that can be played without restrictions on podcasts. Beyond that, they are also starting a "MommyMinute," sort of a tip of the day for mommies.

PART 7

OTHER BLOG
AND PODCAST
CONSIDERATIONS

■ ■ ■

Here you'll find a mix of important blog and podcast topics that don't fit neatly under any one topic, but will be helpful to consider as you navigate the blogosphere.

81. BLOGGING WITHIN A CLASSIC COMMAND AND CONTROL STRUCTURE

Military bloggers

■ ■ ■

It's often said that blogging doesn't mix well with top-down organizations, those with command and control structures. The phrase *command and control* brings the military to mind immediately. If bloggers can offer value within the military, especially within combat zones, then they probably can fit in anywhere. But can they?

There is no official U.S. military viewpoint. The military is trying to evaluate blogging. "The Marines get it; they understand the value of blogging," says Fred Minnick, a veteran who blogged from Iraq and a contributing author to the book *The Blog of War.* Fred reports that the Marines actually encourage blogging. "The Army doesn't get it—maybe they will, maybe they won't." The Army censors blogs within combat zones.

So what's to get? What is it the Marines get that the Army doesn't? Most wars are not only wars on the ground, but information wars as well: wars for the sentiments of the people on both sides of a conflict. A soldier blogging his or her thoughts and feelings is no longer an abstract entity. He or she is a person, and people reading the blog see the soldier, the military, and the entire conflict differently. It's easy to hate an abstract force, but more difficult when this force is made of people, some of whom you may know.

There is also a strong feeling within the military that the mainstream media has an antimilitary bias. "The military sees the mainstream media as being very antisoldier," says Fred. "They only report deaths. They don't report the school openings, food drops, and other humanitarian events." Military bloggers report the good and the bad, and many of them have an enormous following. Americans and Iraqis alike read Fred's blog. Lots of them e-mailed and commented on his blog, and if he didn't post for a few days he'd get lots of "Hope you're OK" type of messages.

Fred blogged anonymously under the pseudonym Sminklemeyer, and his blog is still available and active at *desert-smink.blogspot.com.* He was in public affairs, so he had access to a broad range of information. He was very careful about what he wrote and concentrated on his feelings—for example, how he felt when a friend died, as opposed to facts. "I tried to bring people into my psyche and emotions," explains Fred.

You must tell your commanding officer if you are blogging, supposedly because you might leak sensitive information. However, says Fred, "the real reason the army censors blogs is that they're afraid soldiers will blog about inappropriate things, like reading a book when they are supposed to be on patrol."

Business blogs help personify companies and give them a public face or faces. Military blogs do exactly the same for the armed forces. Business blogs gives businesses a chance to get their message out, as opposed to what the press might report. Similarly, military blogs give the armed forces a chance to tell their side of the story, and are especially important as the military feels the mainstream media is biased against them.

Some businesses don't like the idea of bloggers—they want to control all messages coming from the company. A strong contingent, at least in the Army, feels the same way. Many companies, as well as the Marines, have embraced bloggers because they see their inherent value.

For organizations that think they still control their messages, I've got news for you. You don't anymore—that's just reality. You don't need to embrace blogging or any new media, but you must realize that if you're a sizable organization (military or business), there will always be an underground faction that won't be discovered, and that will have its own messages from within your organization.

82.

BLOGS AND
LEGAL WORRIES

Existing laws that apply to electronic
communications apply to blogs

■ ■ ■

Many companies are concerned with legal issues surrounding blogs. This is not surprising, for blogs are relatively new, and many unanswered legal questions and issues are undecided by courts. In general, though, blogs are just a form of electronic communication and most companies already have electronic communications.

I spoke with John P. Hutchins, a technology lawyer at Troutman Sanders, on legal issues surrounding blogs. Note that I am not an attorney, and this information is for educational purposes only. Legal issues will vary in different locales and countries. Contact your legal counsel for advice that applies to your specific situation. Only broad outlines can be painted in the few words that follow. Additional disclaimers may apply. This information will give you a foundation for understanding the range of legal issues that apply to blogs and blogging.

We can categorize blogs into internal blogs, ones only accessible by company employees, and external blogs, ones accessible from the general Internet.

Internal blogs bring up only a few legal issues. In many ways, internal blogs are similar to e-mail, and existing policies pertaining to electronic communication and document retention may cover blogging adequately. Separate blogging policies are not necessarily required. If internal blogs have anonymous comments, one factor to consider is whether employees have a reasonable expectation of privacy. In general, the answer is no, and many employers make this explicit through their policies.

External blogs have legal issues similar to those associated with other forms of external communications. Uncontrolled bloggers may engage in the following types of conduct:

- Potentially defamatory speech

- Violations of security laws such as disclosing insider information

- Disclosing or threatening to disclose sensitive information, which can range from trade secrets to personal information about company executives

- Threatening conduct

Companies typically have employee policies, codes of conduct and ethics, and contractual agreements with employees to try and control these types of behavior. However, the anonymity of the Internet can embolden employees and nonemployees to engage in this behavior. Anyone can start an anonymous blog and act irresponsibly, and the courts are very deferential to the right to engage in anonymous Internet speech.

Getting the identity of a badly behaved blogger can be extremely difficult, even when his or her identity is known by an ISP or other service provider. Determining the identity of an anonymous blogger may involve a "John Doe" lawsuit against the blogger. And even then, most courts will allow the blogger to defend the suit anonymously until the company makes a convincing argument that its claim has merit, justifying disclosure of the blogger's identity.

Another issue involves potentially defamatory speech in the form of comments, especially anonymous comments, sometimes submitted under a pseudonym. The company may unknowingly become a "publisher" of defamatory speech and incur potential legal liability. Note that the Communications Decency Act provides immunity to ISPs under these circumstances, not bloggers or Web site owners.

If a company censors comments, viewing submitted comments before publishing (typically called comment moderation) or otherwise removing inappropriate comments, any published comments will have been seen by a screener before publishing. This may impose potential liability where none may have existed otherwise, because the act of publishing the comments may be construed as the company approving their content.

Legally and practically speaking, blogs are just another form of electronic communication. Although new issues may arise and need to be decided by the courts, the existing laws that apply to electronic communications apply to blogs.

83.

PROTECTING YOUR
BLOG AND PODCAST
INTELLECTUAL PROPERTY

What exactly do you own?

■ ■ ■

What do bloggers and podcasters actually own? "Intellectual property," says Brett Trout, an attorney who specializes in intellectual property and information technology issues. "Most bloggers and podcasters have a copyright in their content and a trademark on their name and do not even know it." They might even have valuable intellectual property in their domain name or a patentable process in what goes on behind the scenes. "Unfortunately, failure to properly protect intellectual property can cause it to move into the public domain and be lost forever," adds Brett. While patents are expensive, nearly every blog and podcast has the potential for domain name, copyright, and trademark protection.

Domain names are available on a first-come, first-served basis and are inexpensive. For example, if you blog at *bretttrout.wordpress.com,* you may want to get *www.bretttrout.com* sooner rather than later. Although it is illegal to register a domain name that includes someone else's trademark with the intent of profiting from the purchase, "cybersquatting" does occur, and it's best to be proactive and avoid any problems that could occur down the road.

As soon as you use a trademark to identify your posts, you automatically have "common-law" rights in the trademark. You can also obtain federal trademark registration. Common-law rights are important, but a federal trademark registration provides for triple damages and recovery of your attorney fees if someone willfully infringes your trademark. This means defendants usually run scared, rather than fight. You can search the Trademark Office for free at *www.uspto.gov* to make sure that the trademark you want isn't already registered. "While you can register your own federal trademark for a little over $300, paying $1,200 for a trademark attorney to do it right will pay large dividends if you ever have to sue someone for infringement," Brett adds.

You have copyright protection as soon as you post to a blog. "You have to make sure you record a copy of a podcast to have copyright automatically attach," Brett warns. Saving to disk as opposed to just streaming live suffices. "In either case, you need to register the copyright if you ever want to sue anyone for infringing your copyright." Copyright registration covers existing material only, so some people register their copyrights periodically to ensure that new content is also covered. Copyright registration is cheap, because the Copyright Office does not compare your registration against previous registrations. You can do it yourself for about $30, while having a copyright attorney do it runs about $200.

Plagiarism and copyright infringement are sometimes confused. Plagiarism is presenting someone else's work as your own, while copyright is the author's right to reproduce an original work of authorship. Plagiarism is an academic issue, and copyright is a legal issue. Copying *The Da Vinci Code* and publishing the copy as your own, would be both plagiarism and copyright infringement. Copying the *Magna Carta* and presenting it as yours would be plagiarism, but would not constitute copyright infringement, for there is no longer an enforceable copyright on the *Magna Carta.* Conversely, incorporating large, properly cited excerpts from *The Da Vinci Code* in your own novel wouldn't be plagiarism, because you are not claiming the work as your own, but might constitute copyright infringement if you were reproducing the copyrighted work without permission.

Meeting with an intellectual property attorney experienced in working with bloggers and podcasters can help you determine what you have and how to protect it. The information in this book is not legal advice, and it's wise to meet with an intellectual property lawyer; first meetings are often free. "Even if you decide not to go any further, it is a good idea at least to find out exactly what you own and your options for protecting your intellectual property," says Brett. Hmmm, I notice Brett offers a free consultation. I wonder if he'd mind if I podcast our conversation. . . .

84. BLOGS AND SECURITY

Issues to consider

■ ■ ■

"Companies often start blogs without any regard to security issues. I sometimes see this even in very security-conscious companies," says Pierre Noel, president and CEO of the Arial Group, *www.arialgroup.com,* an enterprise risk-management solutions provider. "There are three issues that need to be considered," continues Pierre, "blog software, blog data, and employee actions."

"If a company is considering hosting blog software on their site, for example WordPress or Movable Type, they need to test the software before deploying it," cautions Pierre. It needs the same level of testing as any other software running in the network, especially if it accessible over the Internet, i.e., not used for an internal blog only. Companies sometimes err in thinking that blog data is not that important and thus blog software is not that important, but any insecure software can allow a hacker to gain a foothold and compromise your entire network.

If you are using a hosted solution such as *www.TypePad.com* or *www.Wordpress.com,* there are fewer concerns, but a hacker could still potentially change your blog data—for example, by putting up false or embarrassing posts.

Blogs contain a fair amount of data, primarily posts but also the page's template, as well as information in any sidebars and header. Bloggers often spend untold time generating valuable content, but never consider backing it up. One blog network lost all its data for all its blogs—archived posts and all—recently, because it didn't have backups. It can never hurt to back up your blog data as frequently as you can.

"We need some sort of rules or guidelines for employees," recommends Pierre, both to protect the company and to protect employees. Typically, this document, called a "blogging policy," will often include statements telling employees they must act professionally, not use profanity, etc., and will contain very blog-specific information. "Technically, a blogging policy is part of a company's security policy, which is documentation on the company's security stance," says Pierre, "but what is most important is that blogging policy is approved at a high level, and is well known and easily accessible by employees."

I asked Pierre about concerns that employees would blog confidential information—a popular worry among some management. Pierre just laughed, saying, "Employees blogging confidential information is an employee problem, not a blogging problem. Presumably, the security policy already has rules about that, and they need to be enforced."

There are some security concerns with blogs. Companies need to confirm the software has appropriate security for their needs, and different companies will have different needs. Blog data, including posts, need to be backed up. Finally, a set of rules or guidelines on blogging is necessary to protect the company and its employees.

85.

YOUR BLOG AND YOUR LIVING BRAND

Blogging reveals your essence

■ ■ ■

"Blogging is a free sample of your brand," according to Mike Wagner, president of the White Rabbit Group, *www.whiterabbitgroup.com,* who works with creative brand ownership. A blog allows people to hear your distinct voice and experience your natural enthusiasm for your subject. Blogs allow people to learn about you in a way that won't come through in a speech or a sales call.

Why are you not a commodity—with resulting commodity pricing? Without branding, you, your products, and your services are a commodity. Blogs show what is different about you. "Your difference and relevance is 'out there' for the world to see," stresses Mike. "It shows how you put your unique fingerprint on your business." People get to know you through your blog. Assuming they like you, "It makes you safe to talk to, learn about, and ultimately engage in some sort of business relationship," adds Mike.

Blogs allow potential customers, clients, and partners to see your expertise conveyed through your personality. "This tells them a lot; this is a massive advantage," adds Mike. "It can turn a big, cold corporation into a human being . . . but it can also reinforce that you are a big, cold corporation with no capacity for conversation."

Blogging shows your living brand, your current evolving brand. Old friends and colleagues you reconnect with through your blog, and all other visitors, see the current you and your brand. They may see your blog, for example, and subconsciously think, "He was a mainframe guy when I knew him before, now he's a Microsoft guy."

Blogging allows brand expansion by uncovering hidden value and talent that you may have never known you had. Blogging exposes hidden values and opportunities. Mike was affirmed as a public speaker, and now he's affirmed as a writer. He's been asked to write at *www.MarketingProfs.com*. He never expected that from blogging. Mike adds, "Blogging is kicking me out of my comfort zone into a wonderful space where I am growing, meeting new people, and discovering new opportunity."

Blogging shows what's special and different about you. It shows your expertise and your personality. It emphasizes why you are not a commodity. It is your living brand.

86. ANONYMOUS BLOGGING

Pros and cons

■ ■ ■

Steven Ustaris is passionate about his work and blogs passionately about it as well. He is an associate media director at Carat Fusion, a communications agency, and is fully immersed in advertising. He has strong opinions on many topics, including the use of new media such as blogs and podcasts, and expresses his thoughts freely, as most successful bloggers do.

Unlike most bloggers, however, Steven blogs anonymously. There isn't a hint of his identity on his blog, and it can't easily be traced to him. Of course, it is still possible someone will recognize him, although, unless they know Steven well or he accidentally reveals identifying information, it is unlikely. Many bloggers aren't in favor of anonymous blogging—they think all bloggers should be transparent and hide nothing, especially not their identities. But blogging anonymously provides some bloggers with the space to state opinions that they may not have otherwise expressed.

Steven's anonymity gives him complete freedom. Some of his opinions may run counter to the opinions of Carat Fusion's many customers', and some customers may care. Steven doesn't have to worry. Blogs also invite criticism: When Steven was writing an online cartoon in 1996, one reader took issue with his opinions and sent him a series of personal attacks and threats via e-mail. If he had been writing anonymously, he would have had no worries. Today, no criticism can be directed at him or at his company.

Steven says anonymous bloggers can build popularity. For example, MiniMicrosoft, *minimsft.blogspot.com,* allegedly an anonymous Microsoft insider who rants on Microsoft's problems and how to fix them, is enormously popular. Steven's blog is relatively popular as well, despite his anonymity. His close friends know he's the author, but he has many other readers who don't know his true identity.

Building credibility as an anonymous blogger is more difficult, Steven admits. Typical bloggers put their credibility on the line every time they blog, as well as their companies' names and reputations if they're business bloggers. A company connection brings along some credibility even if the company is not well known. An anonymous blogger, on the other hand, has to build his or her credibility from the ground floor up, one post at a time. Because he or she is risking nothing, building credibility is harder and takes longer.

Blogging anonymously has other shortcomings when compared to "traditional" blogging. Bloggers can be enormous assets to their companies and bring great credibility and visibility, but not if they are anonymous. Blogs sometimes produce business leads and are an additional source of networking, but not if they are anonymous. A business simply cannot receive direct business benefits from an anonymous blog.

Anonymous blogging has many of the benefits of traditional blogging, and one strong advantage—complete freedom. For now, that complete freedom to explore ideas and hold conversations is compelling to Steven, and, obviously, to the other anonymous bloggers out there.

87.

BLOGGING IN
THE CLASSROOM

Creating community through blogging

■ ■ ■

"I have 22 students, and for the first time in teaching in 25 years, everyone is participating, and engaged, and enjoying learning," says Delaney J. Kirk, PhD, professor of management at Drake University. Delaney is talking about her Master of Business Administration class on Managing Diversity in the Workplace.

What's she doing differently that she hasn't done during the proceeding 25 years? She "decided to add a class blog [*delaney.typepad.com/managingdiversity*] to the course as a way of allowing the students to take more ownership of the class and of their own individual learning as together we build a collaborative learning community." Delaney first started blogging about her work helping other college professors become better teachers and classroom managers, and decided to try a class blog as well.

Delaney posts three times a week to the class blog, and students, as part of their class participation, read the blog and add comments. So far, everyone is commenting, and the comments tend to be a paragraph or longer, well thought out, and intelligent. Students are also commenting on other students' comments, and the blog has created a real learning community. This model is a contrast to the twice-weekly class sessions, in which only perhaps five to seven students actively participate. "I'm making it up as I go," says Delaney, but clearly her experiment is wildly successful.

Currently, Delaney is the only poster, although everyone in the class leaves comments. She will probably open it up and allow students to write their own posts in the near future.

So, do the blog conversations parallel the class sessions? Not necessarily. Although some of the posts and resulting discussions do follow from classroom material, Delaney feels free to post on any relevant topics and then watch the ensuing conversation. Sometimes she posts on somewhat controversial topics to get the students talking.

"I'm thinking this is the future of teaching!" adds Delaney, and it's clear that this is working for her and for her students.

88. FRIDAY SQUID BLOGGING

A blog can be professional and still have fun

■ ■ ■

"Squids have personality," reads Schneier on Security, *www.schneier.com/blog,* Bruce Schneier's blog, or "at least the Southern Dumpling Squid does." Bruce is an internationally renowned security technologist and author of numerous books on security. Bruce has taken up "Friday Squid Blogging"—he has decided to supplement his blog with information about squid each Friday.

Squid blogging is Bruce's take on "Friday Cat Blogging." Friday Cat Blogging began several years ago when otherwise serious bloggers decided to drop everything and post pictures of their cats on Fridays, for no particular reason other than to have some fun.

So why Friday squid blogging, Bruce? "More for the whimsy than any other deep-felt psychological reason," says Bruce. "It's fun, it's different, and I've previously used squid in some examples at cryptography conferences, so there's some history, too." Bruce has been squid blogging since the first Friday of 1996 and has "about a dozen squid posts lined up—it's the easiest part of my blogging," he says.

Readers' reactions have been largely positive, with many readers leaving pro-squid comments. Some readers of Bruce's blog have been confused as well, and just don't get it. "I think it's obvious," he says: Bruce is simply having fun. Only one reader has commented negatively, wanting Bruce to get back to posting on security, but the squid blogging doesn't replace entries about security. Bruce has just as much security content as before, and has added more material in the form of posts on squid.

So what's in Bruce's blog's future? He'll still have interesting and timely security information no matter what. He's not sure if he'll continue Friday squid blogging next year or not, but if he doesn't, he'll replace it with something else interesting. He's also considering doing an on-topic Saturday cartoon.

If you've plenty of good focused content, as Bruce does, you can add some of whatever you want, within reason. Bruce's experience shows that a dedicated audience is willing to go along with a blogger who just wants to have a little fun.

89. PASSION, PROFIT, AND MYYAWP

The importance of passion

■ ■ ■

Jeff Wourio and Craig Kasnoff, cofounders of MyYawp, have looked at countless blogs and Web sites, "but few stand head and shoulders above all the rest," says Jeff. They decided it's passion—a real fire in the belly—that separates the really good and compelling sites. Jeff and Craig are passionate themselves—passionate about helping others get their passions out there, and it shows on their Web site, *MyYawp.com.*

So, what is MyYawp? The term originally came from a poem written more than a century ago:

I too am not a bit tamed, I too am untranslatable,
I sound my barbaric YAWP over the rooftops of the world.
—Walt Whitman

These words talk about the importance of passion. "Not just passion—the full, undiluted expression of passion," *MyYawp.com* says. "A Yawp truly is—passionate, yes, but also practical, personal, and powerful on any number of levels." Jeff and Craig believe that the Internet needs more Yawps.

So, once again, what exactly is *MyYawp.com?* "It's a tool that helps people who want to build blogs and Web sites and inject passion and persuasion," says Jeff. "The underlying passion drives success." MyYawp helps in a number of ways, but mainly:

- MyYawp helps people find what they are truly passionate about. "For example, someone may say they are passionate about sports, but in reality they are passionate about baseball relief pitchers," say Jeff.

- MyYawp helps people in "really focusing on that passion." This includes finding others who share your Yawp—your audience—and creating and sharing content that conveys your passion.

What about profit? Is this part of MyYawp? "Profit depends on the person involved—it may be important or not," says Jeff. The MyYawp Web site has information on how to profit from your Yawp. "Passion is very effective for profit," adds Jeff. Passion leads to more Internet traffic and repeat visitors. If you're writing about something you're truly passionate about, your passion will shine through, even if you don't know it, and excite people.

The examples on MyYawp include five blogs and a Web site, and the passion shines through in every one. Jeff and Craig are passionate about helping others get their passions out there. Right now they are working to acquaint people with the concepts, and eventually they hope to make money from it.

MyYawp.com ends appropriately with the following words:

> ***This Above All:***
> *Never lose sight of the passion that drives your Yawp. No matter if your Yawp changes or stays the same, make it an ongoing expression of your heart and mind. Now go out there and Yawp and make your voice heard around the world!*
> *Are You YAWPING?*

The most successful blogs and Web sites are written by people who are passionate about their topics. Blog well, focus on something you're passionate about, and watch your traffic soar!

90. CRISIS MANAGEMENT AND BLOGS

What can companies do when a crisis hits?

■ ■ ■

"Since the spread of information is at lightning speed, you need to react at lightning speed. Actually, you need to be prepared for a crisis. Do your employees know how to respond? How about your corporate bloggers? What if the crisis erupts during the weekend?" asks Tom Taulli. "With the ease of the Internet, bad news can spread like a virus—exacting much damage to your company."

Tom is no neophyte when it comes to crises: he's started and run several businesses, and "needless to say, every day seems to have a crisis." Tom is also a blogger and a columnist at *Forbes.com.* Of course most crises are dealt with internally, "but sometimes the crisis hits the public and you have quick decisions to make. What if a negative article comes out? What if your product is buggy? What if there is misinformation?"

Tom speaks from experience, both his own and his clients'. He recently was the subject of a blog attack. The original blogger who attacked him was not working with accurate information. Tom adds, "Even though I was able to deal with it, and, in the end, I was able to get an apology for the whole thing, the negative message initially spread quickly." Tom wasn't at fault, but what if you are? What if a company truly did blunder? How can blogging help?

Tom gives a great example—*Salesforce.com,* a leading provider of customer-relationship management software that is delivered over the Internet. Companies rely heavily on this software, so their service must be almost perfect. Unfortunately, the company "had some outages, which affected some of its users. Of course, the bloggers quickly spread negative sentiments," says Tom. Instead of doing the typical corporate thing and reporting it was "doing everything possible" to ameliorate the situation, *Salesforce.com* took another approach. "They were honest about the situation and recognized the problem—through blogs." To show how serious they were, they were completely transparent with their customers and set up a Web site at *trust.salesforce.com.* Basically, this shows in real-time how well the *Salesforce.com* online system is performing. In a way, *Salesforce.com* was able to turn a negative situation into a positive portrayal of the company.

Tom believes that blogs are useful in giving a company's viewpoint in a crisis. "I think companies should think broadly. The beauty of a blog is that it is a Web page. In other words, you can use charts, pictures, and even videos. For example, in the case of *Salesforce.com,* having a chart of how reliable the system is can be quite powerful."

If a blogger is spreading negative messages about your company, Tom recommends you "engage with the blogger. I would definitely not be hostile. That is likely to result in much more damage." Engaging with the blogger may result in a new ally. If you are up front and willing to spend time discussing the issues, the blogger may get a better perspective on the company. "Another approach is to post a comment on the blogger's site. Again, be professional and straightforward," recommends Tom. "Keep in mind: Whatever you say may—is likely to—be blogged. So make sure it's something you want for public consumption."

Monitoring the blogosphere "must be part of the crisis management plan. It's ironic, but many companies do not know they have a crisis. They do not realize what many passionate people are saying about their company's products and services," says Tom.

91. BLOG OR E-ZINE?

What should you do?

■ ■ ■

E-zines and blogs are both effective mechanisms for broadcasting news and ideas. What should a typical business do? Are blogs and e-zines always complementary or simply overkill?

E-zine is a contraction of "electronic magazine," and e-zines are short magazines or newsletters sent via email. Many companies publish e-zines and have sign-up forms on their Web sites. The majority of e-zines are free, and many companies even offer freebies such as special reports to encourage people to subscribe.

I didn't need to go far to get an opinion based on lots of experience. The experts from the Blog Squad, Denise Wakeman and Patsi Krakoff, PsyD, two well-known blog experts, see blogs and e-zines as complementary. "Using a blog and an e-zine will help attract more visitors, who become subscribers, who will eventually become clients," according to the Blog Squad.

"Blogs are informal, friendly, and conversational. Blog posts show your personality," say the Blog Squad. Readers get to know who you are and are more likely to engage your services. Posts also can be more current and shorter than in e-zines. Because readers can leave comments, you tend to build rapport with them.

"Blogs link to other blogs and Web sites, which helps you create a viral marketing system, increasing exposure to search engines," adds the Blog Squad. Search engines love blogs!

E-zines are more formal, are less frequently published than blog posts, and showcase your knowledge. When an e-zine is combined with a blog, readers are exposed to your expertise and they get to know you. You may already have an e-zine, and there is no reason not to complement it with a blog.

E-zine delivery is also sometimes stopped by overaggressive e-mail spam filters, but blogs are not impacted.

In an e-zine, links to products, advertisements, and affiliate programs can annoy readers and even cause them to unsubscribe. In a blog, these can all be in the sidebar—perfectly visible and effective, yet less intrusive and less likely to annoy readers.

You could even use a blog to easily put back issues of your e-zine online. I know plenty of businesses that don't have their e-zines online, often because it involves modifying the Web site (and possibly paying someone to do it). With a blog, these concerns go away as each individual e-zine issue can simply be posted—no specialized knowledge is necessary.

The Blog Squad thinks of the Web as a fishpond. "The more fishing lines in the pond, the more fish you are going to catch!" Web site, e-zine, blog—all three are effective, and all three are complementary.

92. THE ROI OF BLOGGING

Sometimes, but not always, difficult to explain

■ ■ ■

John Cass, director of blogging strategies for Backbone Media, *www.backbonemedia.com,* admits that the return on investment (ROI) of blogging is sometimes difficult to explain, but that's because the ROI is not in just one area but in several. And he points out that companies that have been blogging seemingly forever, like Microsoft and Macromedia, certainly know they are receiving ROI. This is further complicated as blogging takes little investment in money, but does require a significant investment of time, and many employees blogging are investing at least some of their personal time as well as company time.

One area in which blogging has ROI is in search engine optimization (SEO). Backbone Media recently conducted research on 140 progressive companies to evaluate their search engine marketing practices. The average company spent $21,000 per month in Google Advertising, with some spending as much as $251,000 monthly. Between the 140 companies, they spent $36 million per year.

Serious money is spent on search engines, and blogging has very demonstrable positive effects on search engine placement. John concurs that "great blogging translates into great search engine rankings." In part this is because of the social nature of blogging, which encourages linking, and search engines love links. Another reason is that blogs make it easy to develop content and, once again, search engines love new content.

Blogging is also great for communications and building brands, yet another area in which companies spend a lot of money. Blogs are easy and very effective ways for product companies to get information out to customers. They are also effective ways to obtain honest customer feedback, arguably more accurate than surveys or focus groups.

"Not every company is a good candidate for blogging," says John. "Do they want to talk about the issues in their industry? If not, blogging may be counterproductive. It also depends on what they're comfortable doing within their corporate culture," adds John. If there is no community of bloggers within the industry, they will need to start from scratch. It'll be harder to get links and readers. Conversely, if a blogging community eventually starts up in their industry, they will be at the forefront.

Companies who have been blogging long term don't worry about the ROI of blogging any more than they worry about the ROI of telephones— they know they are receiving benefits. Many companies that blog or that are considering it won't worry about the ROI, because they see the benefits of other companies' blogs. That said, not every company should blog, but certainly the numbers of blogging companies will increase in the future.

93. NO SITTING AROUND AND WAITING FOR DEMONSTRABLE ROI

All business decisions involve risk

■ ■ ■

Jim Curtin laughs when he hears people question the ROI of blogging. Jim is the president and CEO of Win4Lin, *www.win4lin.com,* and has been described as a serial entrepreneur. His drive, passion, and intuition often amaze me. "Sometimes you've just got to do what feels right," insists Jim. "An entrepreneurial or guerrilla approach does not involve sitting around and waiting for others to follow. If everyone sat around and waited for demonstrable ROI, Amazon wouldn't be selling books on the Internet, Google wouldn't have a search engine, and Henry Ford wouldn't have tried to compete with horses. Where was the provable ROI there?"

Jim stresses that every business decision involves risk. This includes every pricing, marketing, and product decision, as well as the decision to join the blogosphere. It's risky for Microsoft and Coke to be in China, but if they weren't, they would be missing out on a huge market opportunity. Some risks simply have to be taken. For some companies, the decision *not* to blog is extremely risky.

Jim understands that many companies may not see the ROI in blogging and that it may not be appropriate for many to dive in, but the ROI of blogging is clear to his company. "The whole thing is so viral, it's eclipsed the press in terms of getting our word out," says Jim. "The mainstream press doesn't care about your press releases or doing a product review—at least not for smaller companies."

Jim sees the blogosphere "like its own big organism with individual blogs as cells." Win4Lin communicates with the individual cells, often offering sample software to bloggers. Reviews, news, and any other comments flow through the blogosphere from those individual cells. Small companies, at least, should be "really focused on blogs—it's the center of the universe for your buzz and your identity." Win4Lin's products are all over the blogosphere.

Win4Lin is a high-tech company; they have solutions to help businesses facilitate their Linux migration while leveraging their existing investment in Microsoft Windows. This is a hot area, and there is a huge number of high-tech blogs—this makes Jim's decision to focus on blogs a clear one.

Do Jim or Win4Lin blog themselves yet? Jim has a personal blog and is very familiar with the medium. His professional blog is currently in the planning stages and may be live by the time you read this. Jim stresses that you don't need a blog to join the blogosphere and benefit. "Do you need to be an author to benefit from books? Do you need to make movies to enjoy watching them?" he quips.

94.

THE PROMISE
OF VIDEOBLOGGING

Video's barriers to entry are gone

■ ■ ■

Successful blogs extrude personality. If you meet a great blogger, he or she is often just what you'd picture from reading his or her blog. Podcasts take this to another level: Listening to someone's voice, especially on a regular basis, greatly increases the feeling of familiarity that listeners feel. Videoblogging, sometimes also called *vlogging,* takes that feeling to an entirely new level, says Ryanne Hodson, coauthor of the book *Secrets of Videoblogging.* She even met her boyfriend through videoblogging.

Ryanne has a background in video as a video, film, and performance major. She worked for WGBH public television in Boston and even had her own public-access show, but she stresses that videoblogging is easy and anyone can do it. No technical smarts or specialized knowledge are required. Equipment is cheap and easy to operate. Your cell phone may even be able to shoot the video you post to your videoblog.

"Video on the Web is growing rapidly," says Ryanne. Lots of sites will host free video, including the popular YouTube, *www.youtube.com.* But mere video does not make a videoblog. A videoblog has regularly added video content produced by the same person or people, unlike a free-for-all site such as YouTube, and a videoblog allows for feedback, usually in the form of comments. Viewers gain familiarity from a videoblog that grows over time. "Videoblogging is growing at a steady rate," according to Ryanne, but not so fast as general video on the Web.

There is a lot of potential for business to use videoblogging. Imagine a store that regularly videoblogs—you see the store, the employees, their merchandise, etc. When you eventually visit the store, you'll feel pretty comfortable, and the videoblog may mean that you're much more likely to visit the store at all. You're already familiar with the employees and their personalities as well as the layout of the store.

The professional uses of videoblogging haven't been fully explored. A few politicians have taken up videoblogging, including Andrew Rasiej, a candidate for New York City Public Advocate, Senator John Edwards, and Boston City Councillor John Tobin. There is the well-known Microsoft Channel 9 Video Blog. Amanda Congdon, former host of Rocketboom, a satirical news show and probably the most popular videoblog, aired the first commercial ever in this medium for a reported $40,000.

Not so long ago, producing a video was expensive and videos over the Internet were out of the question for most people. Today it's simple and cheap—anybody and any company can do it. Videoblogging is just starting to be used by business, but its possibilities are immense.

95. "PITCHING" BLOGGERS AND PODCASTERS CORRECTLY

Appropriate blogger and
podcaster–public relations interaction

■　■　■

"The more something appeals to a specific community, the more important blogs are for publicity," says Mark Fortier, vice president and director of publicity for Goldberg McDuffie Communications, a public relations firm for publishers, authors, and books. The first step is to identify the right blogs, and this list increasingly includes podcasts as well. The authors Mark represents may know people who blog. They may need to ask their friends and colleagues if they blog. The search engines are also great for finding appropriate blogs. In five minutes you can find the top blogs in any community, and blogrolls are also great sources for finding additional blogs.

Many bloggers like to review books in their areas of interest, and these blogs with established book coverage are ideal candidates. Other blogs can be difficult, for some bloggers are wary of people who work in the PR field. "It's important to tread carefully," warns Mark. "If the author has time and is willing, he or she should be the one contacting bloggers." Unfortunately, many authors are unwilling or unable to do this. The person contacting the blogger has to be familiar with the blog—he or she needs to read it! Mark says that he simply explains he has something the blogger may be interested in, explains why, and politely offers a review copy. If he's been reading the blog and leaving occasional and appropriate comments, this approach works even better. Sometimes the book author even becomes a regular reader of the blog.

"Timing is also important," says Mark. "Bloggers like to feel important." Mark likes to send bloggers review copies about two to four weeks before the book is released.

Journalists read a lot of blogs and are sometimes likely to review a book if there is buzz in the blogosphere. A lot of publicity with the mainstream media involves getting through gatekeepers, and bloggers do that extremely well.

"Blogs are about conversations, and you want to start new conversations," says Mark. "The more something has a new or contrarian view, the more likely bloggers will like it because it'll cause conversation." Books often have a new angle on a subject, so they are ideal fodder for these conversations.

Mark also encourages his authors to start blogs whenever appropriate. There is a time commitment involved, and some authors simply do not have the time. "Also, to succeed you need strong opinions," says Mark. "I can tell within five minutes if someone will make a good blogger."

Mark's techniques make sense regardless of what is being promoted: books, industrial goods, animal husbandry products, or lawn-care services. The basic ideas are to be nice and respectful, and offer something potentially useful. Establish a relationship, and don't merely "pitch."

96. GHOST BLOGGING

Ghostwriting is accepted in many areas,
so why not blogs?

■ ■ ■

"Why does the concept of ghost blogging horrify so many people?" asks Mikal Belicove, a blog strategist and ghost blogger. Most sports figures and celebrities don't write their own books, a great many speeches are not written by the speakers who deliver them, and most quotes from CEOs and presidents in press releases were never actually uttered by them. They contain their thoughts and opinions, but they generally are written by ghostwriters, speechwriters, and PR agency personnel.

"For many people, ghost blogging flies in the face of the authenticity of blogging," says Mikal, "until I mention how speechwriters typically meet with their clients and target their words and thoughts toward the target audience." Speakers are typically chosen for their expertise, not because they are good speechwriters. Speechwriters, on the other hand, are experts at formulating ideas into effective spoken sentences. Ghost blogging is no different. It's the blogger's thoughts and opinions that are important, while the ghost blogger is simply someone good at blogging.

Mikal ghost-blogs for a number of CEOs. He typically talks to his clients for 15 minutes to an hour a day and then drafts their posts. The clients perform the final edits, approve the content, and hit the publish button for each of their posts. The posts contain their thoughts and words, not Mikal's. "Many CEOs find it easier to edit than to write," adds Mikal; his services help them jump-start the process of articulating their ideas.

Most of Mikal's clients usually have a sense of what they want their blogs to do for them, but are unfamiliar with the mechanisms. They often have an ultimate goal that goes beyond sharing their thoughts and expertise. Goals can very widely, but might include establishing thought leadership, running for public office, becoming a well-known speaker in a given industry, or getting published.

Although Mikal offers a full range of blogging services, none of them are turnkey. The client is always involved. He often creates the actual blogs—from scratch, not reusing any templates or images—and drafts posts, but the clients are always actively involved in determining their editorial calendar and explaining to Mikal what they want to say.

Mikal also offers personalized blog monitoring services. He spends up to an hour a day for clients searching for relevant blogs and posts they might want to comment on. He rarely drafts comments, but when he does, it's always after a discussion with the clients on what they want to say, and they always edit the comments and always do the actual publishing.

Mikal adds, "Hiring a ghost blogger is not an easy way out." He might perform 75 percent of the work, but it's still the CEOs' thoughts, opinions, and words, and they provide the essential 25 percent of the input. It's the thoughts and opinions that matter, not the mechanism for getting them into the blogosphere.

97. I USE A GHOST BLOGGER

And it's a secret I'm not ashamed of

■ ■ ■

I managed to interview one of Mikal's ghost-blogging clients. He created a blog and posted once, but then never posted again before hiring Mikal.

Now he posts three times a week. He says, "It takes me about an hour and a half each week to do those three posts with my ghost blogger. I think if I had to do all of the work rather than come up with the ideas and thoughts, I would at a minimum triple my time needed." He does the final edits on all posts and pushes the actual publish button, as do all of Mikal's clients.

He does not advertise that he uses a ghost blogger. The thoughts and opinions he blogs are all his own, but "blogging in general is very concerned with authenticity, and it seems that ghost blogging being public knowledge kills that credibility." He sees a parallel with ghostwritten books. Although certainly far more accepted, ghost authors are looked down upon and their authorship is rarely made public. As blogging becomes more mainstream, ghost blogging may become more accepted, but ghost bloggers will probably stay hidden.

Other advantages are provided by the ghost blogger. He or she provides insight and clarity in taking ideas from a rough format and working them into a post that makes sense and has value. Unlike his client, Mikal writes professionally and understands the blogging medium extremely well.

The client wouldn't do anything differently if he were starting to blog now. Using a ghost blogger is working extremely well for him. He stresses that they have a great system, including current posting and planning on topics and ideas for the future.

He is very happy with his ongoing ghost-blogging experience and adds, "I think that for a lot of very busy CEOs and people like myself, ghost blogging is an extremely valuable way to go. It's the same if I tried to write a book; I wouldn't have the time. I have the ideas and experiences, but not the time. Same for blogging. It's a great setup." Like Mikal, his client agrees that blogging is about getting your ideas out there, and ghostwriting done right can be considered mere mechanics.

PART 8

THE FUTURE

■ ■ ■

The future is hard to predict, but it is clear that blogs, podcasts, and other social media are evolving, and changing the landscape, rapidly. How much lasting effect or where we are going next is anyone's guess. The following four learned people have their own ideas about what the future might bring; draw your own conclusions, or jump into the blogosphere, stick around, and see for yourself.

98. THE FUTURE OF BLOGGING

What can we expect?

■ ■ ■

"Nobody has any idea," says Shel Israel, coauthor of *Naked Conversations* and a business consultant. "But I can tell you what we can expect in the workplace. We're ending the first period of wild hysteria about blogging," adds Shel. When a new Fortune 500 company starts blogging, it's still news today. The normalization of blogging is on the way.

Shel describes the beginnings of blogging at the turn of this century, when lots of unemployed software developers were hanging out in coffee shops with free high-speed Internet access. It was an anticorporate environment and the bloggers set up a strong ethical standard of "total transparency," which is still very much present. The technology became so breathtakingly simple that just about anyone could blog. Blogging has evolved and is going mainstream now. "I foresee a day when it will be as commonplace as e-mail, telephone, IM, and other communications." In the near future, Shel believes new employees will be given a desk, phone, e-mail, and a blog.

Shel flashed back to when he used to be a PR guy. He was involved in the launch of Bank of America's Web site. It wasn't particularly amazing or user-friendly by today's standards; about all you could do was download and print out forms to fill in and bring to the bank in person. Shel helped get this "news" into approximately 85 newspapers' business pages—and Bank of America wasn't even the first bank with a Web site. They were the second, and it was still big news! Today a bank or any company having a Web site is not news. Instead, it is expected. The Internet has become a part of life, and its use in business is standard and essential.

Flash-forward ten or so years: The Internet is much more interactive, but "communicating with a company involves a difficult search for an e-mail address hidden on their Web site, and the person known as *info@company.com*'s response starts with 'Do not respond to this message.'" This scenario sounds familiar because it's repeated umpteen times a day.

"Then blogging arrives," says Shel. "There is general understanding that blogging is fundamentally changing how companies communicate and that dialog beats monologue. Blogging is normalizing. It is following the usual adoption trends taught in Marketing 101." As recently as six months ago, blog enthusiasm was greeted by traditional marketers with "horror and hostility. Today, the big-picture premises of the blogging community are already understood and accepted by a large number of traditional market-ers, and other people in large organizations will adapt blogging from what it is today into something different." Shel adds, "The fundamental change is the dialog, not the blog." And because blogging helps customers and companies, the ensuing disruptions to the systems that are currently in place cannot be avoided for very long.

99.   THE FUTURE OF SOCIAL SOFTWARE

Scott Allen on business blogs, podcasts,
videoblogs, and more

■ ■ ■

Scott Allen is the coauthor of *The Virtual Handshake,* a book about the future of blogs and other social software from the business perspective "Blogging is a phenomenon as we cross the chasm," says Scott. And although he admits it's an overused saying, "Everything is converging." In the future, Scott says, we'll have a more integrated experience. Scott men-tions Amazon "plogs" as an example. *Plog* stands for "personal blog"; the customer's Amazon home page displays show blog posts by the authors of books they've expressed an interest in. In the current iteration, authors need to write blog entries specifically for Amazon, which is clunky, but it does provide a direct connection between Amazon users and authors of the books, and users don't navigate anywhere specific to see blog content. It's an integrated part of the Amazon shopping experience for customers who have turned on the feature.

Scott is not as sold on podcasting. "Business audio is a limited market," says Scott, and much of podcasting is business audio—"the fundamental medium is the same." There are certainly some opportunities for podcasting, but not so many as for blogging. Scott argues convincingly that the idea that people will be listening to business or other audio all their waking hours is false. "I like my quiet time, for example while driving," iterates Scott. "The power of blogging is that it puts the consumer in charge." Does podcasting? "We read three times as fast as anyone talks," continues Scott. It's also hard to scan or search podcasts, and follow links.

Scott feels similarly about videoblogging, although he sees some opportunities. "Video is more compelling than audio," says Scott. He sees opportunities in entertainment and "how-to" videos. "We won't see mass hysteria from these videoblogs and podcasts," he believes. They won't be as big as blogging. A lot of the hype is coming from people who missed the beginning of the blogging phenomena and are convinced not to be left behind again."

A lot of social software has the primary purpose of allowing people to "connect" with each other, such as LinkedIn. This will evolve into communities with a shared sense of purpose—"not just connecting." An example is the Value Investors Club, *www.valueinvestorsclub.com,* a self-described "exclusive online investment club where top investors share their best ideas."

So Scott sees convergence, growth in online communities with a shared sense of purpose, text as king—and podcasts and videoblogs as minor players. Text, as opposed to audio or video, leaves the consumer in charge; he or she can scan, read at their own rate—no doubt faster than listening to audio or watching video—search easily, and follow hyperlinks at will.

100. THOSE INVOLVED ARE TOO CLOSE TO SEE WHAT'S HAPPENING

It's a nonmainstream fad with value

■ ■ ■

"It's a fad," says technologically adept and successful Dave Kesel, who currently describes himself as a "surfer and deep thinker." However, "that doesn't mean there isn't any long-term value—there clearly is, but many people have jumped on the bandwagon who will soon jump off." Many people who start a blog or podcast won't keep it up for a year. Dave doesn't blog or podcast and doesn't plan on it, although he is very familiar with the medium, and is happy to share his thoughts.

"Blogging is simply not mainstream yet," says Dave. Most people may have heard the word *blog,* but many can't define it. Some blog readers don't know they are reading a blog, and may not care. "I don't care if it's a blog," says Dave, "what I care about is whether it engages me and provides value, and most people agree."

"Podcasting is even further out," Dave continues. If they've heard of the term, many people think *podcasting* has something to do with iPods. "Podcasts, iTunes, RSS, podcatchers, these terms mean absolutely nothing to the average person," Dave insists, pointing out that plenty of great audio content and music exists aside of podcasts. "I just turn on the radio or put in a CD," Dave says. He doesn't want to "play" with technology and, he says, neither do most people.

"The idea that most people will be blogging or podcasting is just nuts," Dave insists. People have very limited time; they already have full lives with their passions, jobs, families, and more. Dave believes that very slowly people are starting to get more news and entertainment from social media such as blogs and podcasts, but wide-scale acceptance isn't remotely close.

"Bloggers and podcasters are passionate about blogging and podcasting, just like I'm passionate about surfing," Dave says, "They're so passionate that they're unrealistic." Dave would love to be a professional surfer, but that's unrealistic. Few people support themselves through surfing. He says people thinking they'll make money from blogging or podcasting is a similarly unattainable dream. Most of Dave's social interaction outside his business world is with other surfers, just like many bloggers and podcasters interact primarily with other bloggers and podcasters. "It simply gives you a warped view," says Dave.

Dave does believe there is a lot of potential and value in blogging and podcasting and other social media. "Sure, some people are benefiting from it now," Dave says, "but for your average person, the benefit is in the future, not today."

101. BLOGS AND PODCASTS, WHERE DO WE GO FROM HERE?

The democratization of information

■ ■ ■

"The future of blogging and podcasting will empower a planet of information sharing—the individual opinions of citizens, customers, and family members will freely flow and influence all," says Jeremiah Owyang, a global Web strategist who manages New Media Web programs for a global storage solutions company in Santa Clara. He believes three catalysts will enable this evolution: normalization of sharing, ubiquitous publishing, and amorphous content.

Normalization of sharing. "As a society, we'll move away from words such as *'blogs'* and *'podcasts'* as online publishing will become native and second nature," says Jeremiah. As publishing normalizes, many services will organize and access information. Tags, memes, various metadata, and analytics will be used to enable information to be shared quickly and easily.

Sharing this rich information will occur without regard to geographic and corporate boundaries, as well as between disparate groups in society.

Ubiquitous publishing. People will have the freedom to create and access content from any location because of advances in mobile technology, and this will make instant publishing both native and natural. Many Asian cultures already have a strong culture of mobile publishing and communication, publishing rich media from text, pictures, video, and more, and this will eventually become common in other cultures around the globe. Users will be able to access highly accurate information easily and quickly from a cell phone or other portable device.

Amorphous content. Information will not only be available in its raw format, in blogs and podcasts, but will also be repackaged into different combinations and formats. Data streams will be combined, as relevant individual opinions are mixed with those of similar interest. Content will be repurposed to multiple mediums such as TV, radio, Web, and mobile. Real-time language translation services will tear down the language barriers of blog and, eventually, podcast content.

"These three catalysts will enable everyone to create a new online library of the collective," says Jeremiah. "While this information source will be vast, we'll be able to disseminate information in any method we prefer—it can be organized, categorized, searched, streamed, and found in any way we'd like." Blogs and podcasts will be the foundation for news as citizens, consumers, and employees report information in real time.

Information will be shared across territorial, political, and organizational boundaries, and the corporate firewall will become a gray area of communication between employees and customers as a collaborative environment creates new products that meet the exact needs of buyers. The new workforce will bring with them their existing social networks, primarily empowered by social sites such as MySpace, Bebo, and Facebook, and they will maintain and grow these networks as they move across regions, companies, and industries. Extended families will organize across distances—these tools will create rich and detailed archives of our lives. Soon, these will evolve to real time, enabling faster communication.

"In the end, anyone will be able to publish their thoughts, and the opinions of the individual and masses will influence global culture, cement business relationships, and connect loved ones as information is democratized," adds Jeremiah.

EPILOGUE

Web 2.0 represents the new generation of interactive technologies and services, such as blogs and podcasts, that allow people to collaborate and share information online. It is transforming business and society.

I have many good friends I've never met that I regularly communicate with via blogs and e-mail. Many people just one generation older cannot conceive of this. Many grade school kids and teenagers race home to interact with friends over the Web. I also have solid and profitable business relationships with people I've never met and in some cases have never spoken to on the phone. All of these relationships were brought about by blogging and related technologies.

I'm not going to tell you that you need to blog or podcast, or that businesses that don't adopt blogging will become extinct soon. Plenty of businesses may never blog, podcast, or adopt the next new technology.

But what *does* every businessperson need to do? Business is changing rapidly, more so than in most periods of history. You need to pay attention, because whether you consider yourself a part of the blogosphere or not, the rapidly changing technologies that are in use today do affect every corner of the business world.

Watch what's happening with blogs, podcasts, and other emerging media of communication. Pay attention. Listen. Read. And be prepared to act quickly.

AdSense Google's contextual advertising system that allows almost any Web site or blog owner to publish ads and be paid "per click" on the advertisements. AdSense is contextual in the sense that advertisements are automatically chosen based on the text on the Web site or blog.

aggregator Another term for *feed reader.*

Atom One of the many competing formats for feeds. See *feed.*

blog A simple Web site with information displayed in reverse chronological order. Blogs are typically frequently updated, contain opinion and facts much like newspaper editorials, and allow reader feedback in the form of comments.

blog network A collection of blogs that are organized and managed together. Blogs in a network may be collectively or individually owned. Blogs are often organized into networks for the purpose of selling advertising; each individual blog may not have enough traffic to interest advertisers, but the collection of all blogs in the network often will.

blogosphere The community of all blogs, including the links and social interaction between them. Most people include podcasts in their definition of the blogosphere, although occasionally the term *podosphere* is used to refer to the community of podcasts.

blogroll A collection of links to blogs. Many blogs display a blogroll in their sidebars, often titled "Blogs I Read" or "Blogs I Like."

categories Categories are simply subjects a blogger writes about. Most blogging software allows the creation and organization of blog posts by category. This helps readers browse the material in a blog.

comments Although only the author or authors of a blog can post articles, most blogs allow readers to add comments to individual blog posts. Comments allow discussion on blog posts. Comments are typically text but also may be audio or video.

e-zine A contraction of electronic magazine, e-zines are short magazines or newsletters sent via e-mail. Many companies publish e-zines and have signup forms on their Web sites. The vast majority of e-zines are free, and many companies offer freebies such as special reports to entice people to subscribe.

feed A feed allows readers to see what is new or featured on a blog (or Web site) without visiting the Web site. This makes it possible to keep up-to-date on more sites more easily. A feed is implemented as a simple file that contains what is new or featured and is viewed via a feed reader such as MyYahoo! The term *RSS* is sometimes generally used to refer to any feed.

feed reader A feed reader is a utility that reads feeds. They display what is new or featured on blogs and Web sites that users are subscribed to. Feed readers are implemented as standalone or Web-based utilities, or as plugins to an e-mail program or other application.

internal blog An internal blog is a blog that is not publicly accessible. For example, it may be behind a firewall and hence not accessible via the Internet, or it may require a password for access,

iTunes A free and easy-to-use digital media player application from Apple for downloading, playing and organizing music and video files. iTunes is available for Apple and Windows platforms and is often used to subscribe to and download podcasts.

monetize To derive income from. Blogs and podcasts are sometimes monetized via advertising or affiliate programs that pay a commission.

MP3 A popular format for audio files, commonly used for podcast files.

podcast Podcasts are audio posts on blogs with two key characteristics: they have a showlike structure, and users can subscribe and download new content automatically. Podcast blogs are blogs that contain podcasts and supporting material, such as text descriptions.

post A single blog article. The unit of blog publishing. Also used as a verb: "He posted his opinions on the matter to his blog."

RSS One of the competing formats for feeds. There are several incompatible versions in use, and the acronym varies depending on the version. RSS stands for "Rich Site Summary" or "Really Simple Syndication," depending on the version. See *feed*.

sidebar A narrow vertical strip of screen on a blog that contains miscellaneous information, such as information about the author, categories, and date-based archives. Sidebars can be on the right or left side, and some blogs implement multiple sidebars.

social media Software used to share information and collaborate, often over the Internet. Social media includes message boards, blogs, podcasts, and wikis.

trackback Trackbacks are just blog comments, but they are comments left on another blog. The blog commented on via trackbacks will update the original post with a link to every blog that has tracked back, allowing readers to see exactly who has commented on the post and read what they have written. Not all blogging software implements trackbacks.

videoblog A blog where the primary content consists of video.

Web 2.0 Web 2.0 is a catchall phrase that refers to the new generation of interactive technologies and services available on the Web that allow people to collaborate and share information online. Web 2.0 technologies include blogs and podcasts.

wiki A type of Web site that allows multiple users to easily add, remove, and edit content. Wikis are often used for collaborative authoring. Wiki also is used to refer to the collaborative enabling software itself.

Part 1: The Basics

"What Is a Blog?"

Raleigh Design, *www.raleighdesign.us*

Blogging for Business, *BloggingForBusinessBook.com*

Axis Technology, LLC, *www.axistechnologyllc.com*

"Comments—Essential to Blogs?"

Bryper.com, Blogging on new media and online communications, *www.bryper.com*

"Blogging Platforms and Blogging Software"

Gray eMarketing Solutions, *www.gemsolv.com*

"The Three Types of Blogs"

Seth Godin's Blog, *sethgodin.typepad.com*

"The Value of Blogging"

A New Marketing Commentator, *www.anewmarketingcommentator.com*

"Why Should Companies Monitor Blogs?"

Women's New Media, *womensnewmedia.blogs.com*

"One Example of Great Blogging Results"

Humor Power, *www.humorpower.com/blog*

"How Many Readers Do You Need for Success?"

QA QnQ, *www.qaqna.com*

"Dave Taylor on Successful Business Blogging"

Ask Dave Taylor, *www.askdavetaylor.com*

The Intuitive Life Business Blog, *www.intuitive.com/blog*

"What Is a Podcast?"

A "shel" of my former self, *blog.holtz.com*

For Immediate Release, The Hobson & Holtz Report, *www.forimmediate release.biz*

"What Is a Videoblog?"

Vlog Anarchy, *michaelverdi.com/index.php/2005/02/20/vlog-anarchy*

Free Vlog, *www.freevlog.org*

Michael Verdi, *www.michaelverdi.com*

"Introducing Social Media to an Organization"

ProPr, *www.propr.ca*

shift+control, *www.76design.com*

Inside PR, *www.insidepr.ca*

"It's All an Experiment"

infOpinions?, *www.auburnmedia.com/wordpress*

Marcom Blog, *www.marcomblog.com*

Part 2: Some Business Uses of Blogs and Podcasts

"Blogs as Reference Tools"

BlogofBob, *www.rp2c.com/cs/blogs/blogofbob*

"Knowledge Management"

E L S U A ~ A KM Blog, *www.elsua.net*

"Blogs for Local Businesses"

Signs Never Sleep, *signsneversleep.typepad.com*

"Internal Blogs Help Teams Communicate"

Know More Media, *www.knowmoremedia.com*

"Blogs and Public Relations"

Dan Janal's PR Leads Blog, *www.prleads.com/blog*

Dan Janal's Great Teleseminar Tips, *www.greatteleseminars.com/blog*

"Building Great Business Relationships through Blogging"

Phil Gerbyshak Challenges You to Make It Great!, *makeitgreat. typepad.com.*

"Position Yourself as an Expert"

Small Biz Survival, *smallbizsurvival.com*

"Blogging for Business Relationship Quality"

Mothers of Invention, *www.themothersofinvention.com*

Freaking Marketing, *www.freakingmarketing.com*

"Blogs and Podcasts at 800-CEO-READ"

Daily Blog, *www.800ceoread.com/blog*

Excerpts Blog, *www.800ceoread.com/excerpts*

InBubbleWrap, *www.inbubblewrap.com*

ChangeThis, *www.changethis.com*

"Blogs Humanize Companies"

Symmetric Technologies, *www.symmetrictech.com*

"Blogging for a Big Company"

Cyberspace People Watcher, *act2.spaces.msn.com*

Computer Science Teacher, *blogs.msdn.com/alfredth*

"Creating Buzz with Blogs"

Buzzoodle, *www.buzzoodle.com*

"Marketing with Content"

David Meerman Scott, *www.davidmeermanscott.com*

Web Ink Now, *www.webinknow.com*

The New Rules of PR, *www.davidmeermanscott.com/documents/New_Rules_of_PR.pdf*

"Blogging Interns"

e-Bizz by Christopher Salazar, *ebizz.wordpress.com*

"Blogging and Your Career"

The Art and Science of Being an I/T Architect, *artsciita.blogspot.com*

"Book Blogs"

Guerrilla Consulting, *guerrillaconsulting.typepad.com*

"A Blog as a Web Portal"

GMP Training and Implementation Tips, *www.gmptraining systems.blogspot.com*

"CEO Blogs"

BlogWrite for CEOs, *www.BlogWriteForCEOs.com*

"Real Estate Blogs"

Blogging Systems, *www.bloggingsystems.com*

"Lawyer Blogs"

LexBlog, *www.lexblog.com*

Part 3: Planning Your Blog

"Blogs and the Big Picture"

Throwaway blog example, *www.HartsHillHoneys.blogspot.com*

Photo album blog example, *TheCrewsBlog.blogspot.com*

Rick Short's B2B Marcom blog, *www.indium.com/RickShort*

"Three Key Questions to Answer When Planning Your Blog"

Better Business Blogging, *www.betterbusinessblogging.com*

"The Who, How, What, Where, and When of Blogging"

Real Oasis, *www.realoasis.com*

Real Oasis Blog, *www.realoasis.net*

"Five-Plus Tips to a Better Blog"

Meryl's Notes, *meryl.net/section/blog*

"Common Mistakes Professionals Make with Their Blogs"

Build a Better Blog, *www.buildabetterblog.com*

Fix My Blog, *www.fixmyblog.com*

"Quarterly Blog Reviews and Editorial Calendars"

Knee Deep, *advanced-approach.blogs.com/knee_deep*

"Practical Blogging"

Practical Blogging, *www.sleepyblogger.com*

"How to Figure Out the Content Dilemma"

(3i) innovate. integrate. ignite. *3i.wildfirestrategy.com*

"Does Your Blog Stink?"

Why My Blog Stinks, *WhyMyBlogStinks.com*

"Blogs and Podcasts in the Enterprise"

ALL KIND FOOD, Managing & Living with Technology, Media, & Systems, *www.ddmcd.com*

Web 2.0 Management Survey, *www.ddmcd.com/findings*

Part 4: Making Money

"Can I Make Money Blogging?"

Performancing, *performancing.com*

"Tips for AdSense and Other Advertisements"

Elemental Truths, *elementaltruths.blogspot.com*

"E-commerce and Blogs"

Tchvertizing, *www.techvertising.com*

"Shopping Carts for Blogs (and Other Web sites)"

Tom Antion, *www.antion.com*

KickStartCart, *www.kickstartcart.com*

"Creating and Selling Information Products from Your Blog"

copyblogger, *www.copyblogger.com*

"Blog Networks"

Bloglogic.net, *www.bloglogic.net*

"Blogging for a Blog Network"

Know More Media, *www.knowmoremedia.com*

PanAsianBiz, *www.panasianbiz.com*

A Man Walks into an Office, *www.amanwalksintoanoffice.com*

"Passion, Persistence, and Profit"

Boston Sports Media Watch blog, *www.bostonsportsmedia.com*

Part 5: Promoting Your Blog and Tracking Statistics

"Great Bloggers Are Great Conversationalists"

Backbone Media, *www.backbonemedia.com*

Scout, *www.scoutblogging.com*

"Evangelizing Your Blog"

Signum sine tinnitu by Guy Kawasaki, *blog.guykawasaki.com*

"Search Engine Optimization for Blogs"

SEO Book, *www.seobook.com*

"The Blog Traffic King on Building Blog Traffic"

Entrepreneur's Journey, *www.entrepreneurs-journey.com*

Blog Traffic Tips, *www.blogtrafficking.com*

"E-mail Blog Interfaces"

FeedBlitz, *www.feedblitz.com*

"Feeds—Easy, Convenient, and Fast Access to New Content"

Pheedo, RSS+Weblog Marketing Solutions, *www.pheedo.com*

"Tracking Blog Statistics"

BusinessBlogWire, *www.businessblogwire.com*

"Tracking and Optimizing Feeds with FeedBurner"

FeedBurner, *www.feedburner.com*

ConverStations, *www.converstations.com*

Copywriting Watch, *www.copywritingwatch.com*

Part 6: Podcast Specific Topics

"What Makes a Great Podcast"

Paul Gillin's blog—Social Media and the Open Enterprise, *www.paulgillin.com*

"Everyone Should Podcast"

SavvySoloCAST, *www.savvysolocast.com*

Solostream Global Media, *www.savvysolo.com*

"Some Podcasting Advice"

Network Security Blog and Podcasts, *www.mckeay.net*

The Podcast Roundtable, *podcastroundtable.com*

"Talkr—Converting Blogs to Podcasts"

Talkr, *www.talkr.com*

"Monetizing Podcasts"

GrapeRadio, *www.graperadio.com*

Michael's Reel Reviews, *reelreviewsradio.com*

MWG blog, *mwgblog.com*

"What Do Podcast Listeners Want?"

Free Resume And Career Toolbox podcast, FRACAT, *www.fracat.com/blog*

The Podcast Roundtable, *podcastroundtable.com*

"Podsafe Music"

Podsafe Music Network, *music.podshow.com*

PodShow, *www.podshow.com*

Reality Bitchslap, *www.cc-chapman.com*

Accident Hash, *accidenthash.podshow.com*

Managing The Gray, *www.managingthegray.com*

U-Turn Café, *u-turncafe.podshow.com*

"Promoting Your Music through Podcasting"

Brother Love Notes, *www.brotherlovenotes.blogspot.com*

Brother Love's Web site, *www.brotherloverocks.com*

"Waxxi, an Interactive Podcast Model Plus"

Waxxi, *www.waxxi.us*

"The New Rules of Podcasting"

Podcast NYC blog, *www.podcastnyc.net/blog*

Podcast NYC, *www.podcastnyc.net*

"Manic Mommies"

Manic Mommies, *www.manicmommies.com*

"The Financial Aid Podcast"

The Financial Aid Podcast, *www.financialaidpodcast.com*

"Rightlook Radio"

Rightlook Radio, *rightlookradio.com*

"Grape Radio"

GrapeRadio, *www.graperadio.com*

"MommyCast"

MommyCast, *www.mommycast.com*

Part 7: Other Blog and Podcast Considerations

"Blogging within a Classic Command and Control Structure"

In Iraq for 365, *desert-smink.blogspot.com*

"Blogging and Legal Worries"

Troutman Sanders, LLP, *www.troutmansanders.com*

"Protecting Your Blog and Podcast Intellectual Property"

Blawg IT-Internet Patent, Trademark and Copyright Issues with Attorney Brett Trout, *blog.bretttrout.com*

Law Offices of Brett J. Trout, P.C., *bretttrout.com*

"Blogs and Security"

The Arial Group, *arialgroup.com*

"Your Blog and Your Living Brand"

Own Your Brand, *ownyourbrand.com*

The White Rabbit Group, *www.whiterabbitgroup.com*

"Blogging in the Classroom"

Managing Diversity, *delaney.typepad.com/managingdiversity*

Ask-Dr-Kirk, *www.delaneykirk.com*

"Friday Squid Blogging"

Schneier on Security, *www.schneier.com/blog*

"Passion, Profit, and MyYawp"

MyYawp, *www.myyawp.com*

"Crisis Management and Blogs"

Tom Taulli, *www.taulli.com*

"Blog or E-zine?"

Build a Better Blog, *www.buildabetterblog.com*

Fix My Blog, *www.fixmyblog.com*

"The ROI of Blogging"

Backbone Media, *www.backbonemedia.com*

Corporate Blogging Survey Results, *www.backbonemedia.com/blogsurvey*

"No Sitting Around and Waiting for Demonstrable ROI"

Win4Lin, *www.win4lin.com*

"The Promise of Videoblogging"

Ryanne's Video Blog, *ryanedit.blogspot.com*

"'Pitching' Bloggers and Podcasters Correctly"

Goldberg McDuffie Communications, Inc., *www.goldbergmcduffie.com*

"Ghost Blogging"

Mikal Belicove, *www.belicove.com*

Part 8: The Future

"The Future of Blogging"

Naked Conversations, *redcouch.typepad.com*

The Cluetrain Manifesto, *www.cluetrain.com*

Grasshopper Factory, *www.grasshopperfactory.com*

"The Future of Social Software"

The Virtual Handshake Blog, *www.thevirtualhandshake.com/blog*

"Blogs and Podcasts, Where Do We Go from Here?"

Web Strategy by Jeremiah, *www.web-strategist.com*

INDEX

A

Abandoned blogs, 75
"About Me" links, 44
Accessing your blog, 72
Accident Hash, 134, 141
Address book services, online, 45
Adkins, Reg, 90
AdSense, 17, 89, 90–91, 103, 166
Advanced Approach, 77
Advertising/advertisers, 80, 87
    ad/content continuity, 91
    blog networks and, 99–100
    Google AdSense, 17, 89, 90–91,
      103, 166
    lawyers and, 65
    "pay per click," 91
    podcast networks and, 138
    relevancy of, 91
    RSS ads, 117
    tips, 90–91
Aggregating blogs, 37
Allen, Bruce, 102
Allen, Scott, 178–79
Amazon.com, 103, 178
American Family podcasts, 124
Analytics, 181
anewmarketingcommentator.com, 13
Anonymity, 23, 157–59
Antion, Tom, 93–95
Apple Computers, 25
Archive, of blog posts, 4
Arial Group, 155
*Art and Science of Being and I/T
   Architect, The,* 57
Ask Dave Taylor, 21

Associate program capabilities, 95
Atom, 118
Attensa, 37
Attorney blogs, 65–66
Axis Technology, LLC, 5

B

Backbone Media, 107, 166
Ballmer, Steve, 52
Banner, 73
Barron, Randy, 5–6
Baseler, Randy, 51
Bebo, 182
Belew, Bill, 101
Belicove, Mikal, 172
Better Business Blogging, 70–71
b5media, 100
Biographies, of blog authors, 3
Blogads.com, 103
Blogdigger, 37
Blogger *(www.blogger.com),* 9
Blogging for Business (Demopoulos),
   3–4, 10
Blogging Systems, 63
Bloglines, 15, 115, 118
Bloglogic.net, 99
Blog networks, 99–102
Blog of War, The, 149
Blogosphere
    atmosphere, 6
    monitoring, 164
BlogPulse, 14
Blog review, 79
Blogrolls, 44–45, 109, 170